The Drum Mast

A Compact Guide to Musical Expr

BY FLORIAN ALEXANDRU-ZORN

Alfred

Acknowledgements

Florian Alexandru-Zorn would like to thank:

My wife and my children.

Thomas Petzold, and all at Alfred Music Publishing.

Thomas Barth, Karl Heinz Menzel, and all at Sonor Drums.

Norbert Saemann, Stephan Hänisch, and all at Meinl Cymbals.

Joe Testa, Vic Firth, Ben Davis, and all at Vic Firth.

Marco Soccoli, Ben O'Brian Smith, Steve Lobmeier, and all at Evans Drumheads.

Bernd Neubauer, and all at beyerdynamic.

Curt Doernberg from Musik Wein.

Peter Waschke, and all at SPL.

Rainer Blanck, and all at Sommercable.

Jochen Erbacher, and all at König & Meyer.

Alfred Music Publishing
LEARN • TEACH • PLAY

info@alfredverlag.de
alfredverlag.de

Printed in Germany

Cover design: Marco Besler
Photos: Florian Alexandru-Zorn
Engraving: Florian Alexandru-Zorn
English translation: Lindsay Chalmers-Gerbracht
Editing and production: Thomas Petzold

Art.-Nr.: 20219US
ISBN 13: 978-3-943638-52-3

Introduction

This volume is the distillation of all studies I have undertaken up to the present day. I practice these concepts in intricate detail on a regular basis. It has taken me several years to complete the process of writing this book and I am now looking forward to being able to share these practice techniques and concepts with others. *The Drum Master Key* can be utilized within a wide range of styles and is therefore timeless. I consider it essential not to limit the focus to a single genre or playing technique.

Acquiring new vocabulary enriches our own individual mode of expression and simplifies conversation with fellow musicians. We percussionists occupy a special role in music; our primary focus is on rhythm and phrasing and we devote our concentration to these two areas to a substantially greater degree than most other instrumentalists. For this reason, I consider it essential to practice exercises not only within double and triple groups, but also to incorporate quintuplets, septuplets, etc. into our daily vocabulary. This knowledge and the associated "thinking outside the box" will reinforce our playing technique and permit us to become more open-minded for new paths.

Each chapter of *The Drum Master Key* opens a further door to a wide range of musical dimensions. Beginning with fundamental rhythms and dynamics and proceeding to polymeters, displacements, and daily workouts, I have attempted to compile all essential elements for independent practice. I find it fascinating to observe how each individual percussionist has a different sound although we are all united by a single factor: the rhythmic foundation on which all our playing is based. This master key has been conceived for all percussionists, and players are individually free to decide how this material can be best employed to enhance their own personal style.

Children provide us with a good example.

They enjoy playing with building blocks and, depending on their whim of the day, produce the most amazing variety of constructions: towers, castles, dragons, etc. Sometimes they simply build whatever comes into their head.

All utilize the same starting material, but produce different results every time. If you have a precise vision of what you want to play, you will succeed in combining all these building blocks differently everytime with the aid of this book, thereby extending your abilities and learning how to employ them flexibly.

If you do not have a clear picture of what you want to play, I advise you to work systematically through the concepts towards the point at which the previously fuzzy image will gradually come into focus and reveal its clarity.

Now enjoy this musical voyage of discovery!

Florian Alexandru-Zorn

Contents

The Key to Time

The Master Key

The Key to Displacements / Polymetric

Drum Key

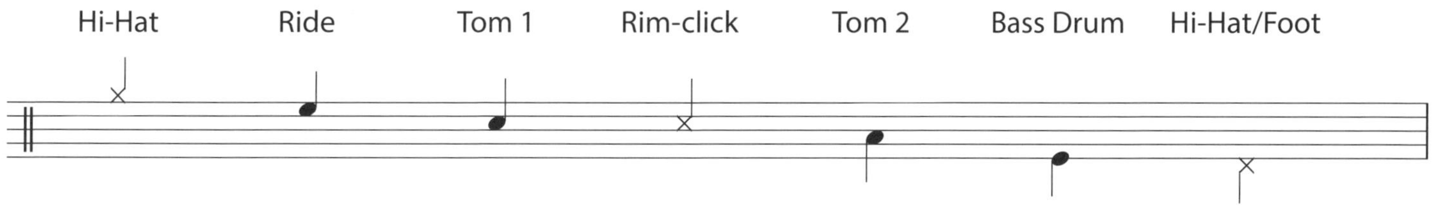

How to Use This Book

It is not important to proceed through this volume in chronological order.

Each chapter is devoted to self-contained work fields that are imperative for all percussionists. A solid foundation always is the ideal basis for a stable learning process—this is provided in the first chapter "**The Key to Time**."

The other chapters can, however, be worked through in any order. It is in fact advisable to jump back and forth between the different chapters to gain new insights into the individual exercises. Where possible, the concepts in this book are deliberately reproduced in tabular form. This means that the individual parts have to be assembled mentally which will in turn ensure that the material is memorized better, and you will be quicker in developing the ability to retrieve this material at any time.

Progress through the exercises one by one and attempt to play through each section until you are able to continue playing even if your attention starts to wander.

According to new scientific studies, the human brain requires around 160 repeated attempts to memorize something permanently. Here this will take around **15–20 minutes** at approx. **100 bpm** per 4/4 bar.

The principle of repetition is, however, only one aspect of reinforcing something that has recently been learned. I attach even greater significance to the question of how the acquired knowledge that is to be used. It is therefore first necessary to know how to go about learning something, but equally important to recognize the purpose of learning.

Here is a concrete example:

Can you remember back to your first day at school or the route you took during your driving test?

Older persons are able to recall situations, emotions, and scents that sometimes go back several decades—how is this possible?

The solution is extremely simple: the intensity of a particular situation. This is not merely dependent on repetition, but also on the individual attitude and associated degree of motivation with which exercises are performed. It is therefore necessary first to recognize why something has to be practiced, as this will make actual practice significantly easier. My guiding principle is that I feel privileged as a musician simply by being able to "play."

The Key to Time

Rhythm and phrasing remain a focal point for percussionists. We want to produce a good groove that enables listeners to share our experience. Even if quintuplets and septuplets are relatively seldom in everyday music, it is still important to devote yourself to these rhythms to consolidate your own general rhythmic skills.

It is possible to devote attention to the following exercise throughout your entire life as a percussionist. This is the key that will enable you to open several doors simultaneously.

If you occupy yourself intensely with this material, you will soon establish that you are able to enhance your own perceptive faculty and freedom of movement step by step. You will find it progressively easier to play your breaks, fills, or linear rhythms without having to think about the stickings; you simply play. If you work your way systematically through this exercise, you will develop ideas that will enrich your own playing style through new rhythms.

Even if you are not familiar with all note values from the **pyramid stickings**, you should first play through each individual bar on your own with a standard sticking pattern such as **RLRL** or **RRLL**.

Once each bar has been mastered on its own, this should be followed by a complete series, from quarters to thirty-second-notes with a single sticking. Here it is important to give yourself time and approach one bar after another. In the next step, the stickings are combined with one another to create your own individual sticking patterns. A good starting tempo is **50 bpm**.

This exercise is relevant for all percussionists from beginners to professionals.

The following tables display all sticking possibilities that are feasible in a row of four consecutive beats. This produces sixteen combination possibilities per table. Combined with one another, this will produce **16 x 16, i.e. 256 sticking variants**. Now you see why this exercise can accompany you for a long time.

The sticking is compiled as follows:

	RL	LR	RR	LL
RL	X			
LR				
RR				
LL				

\+

	RL	LR	RR	LL
RL		X		
LR				
RR				
LL				

= **RLRL RLLR**

Ex.:

Pyramid Stickings

	RL	LR	RR	LL
RL				
LR				
RR				
LL				

	RL	LR	RR	LL
RL				
LR				
RR				
LL				

The Master Key

This chapter is divided into two separate phases in relation to the relevant note value.

1st Phase:

One interpretation concept is selected for each note value as a concrete playing instruction.

2nd Phase:

In the second phase, an interpretation exercise is selected and played through with the subsequent combination possibilities of the individual note values.

For example, an interpretative aspect is selected for working through eighth notes (e.g. accent studies or foot technique, etc.) and this interpretation concept is then worked through with the individual note values.

All interpretation exercises can either be played through individually or combined with each other as desired.

This will produce an endless series of different concepts that can be tailored to individual playing needs.

Each interpretation exercise is designed around the individual note values: rock grooves or bossa nova will for example be employed for eighth notes.

Jazz comping can be found under eighth-note triplets.

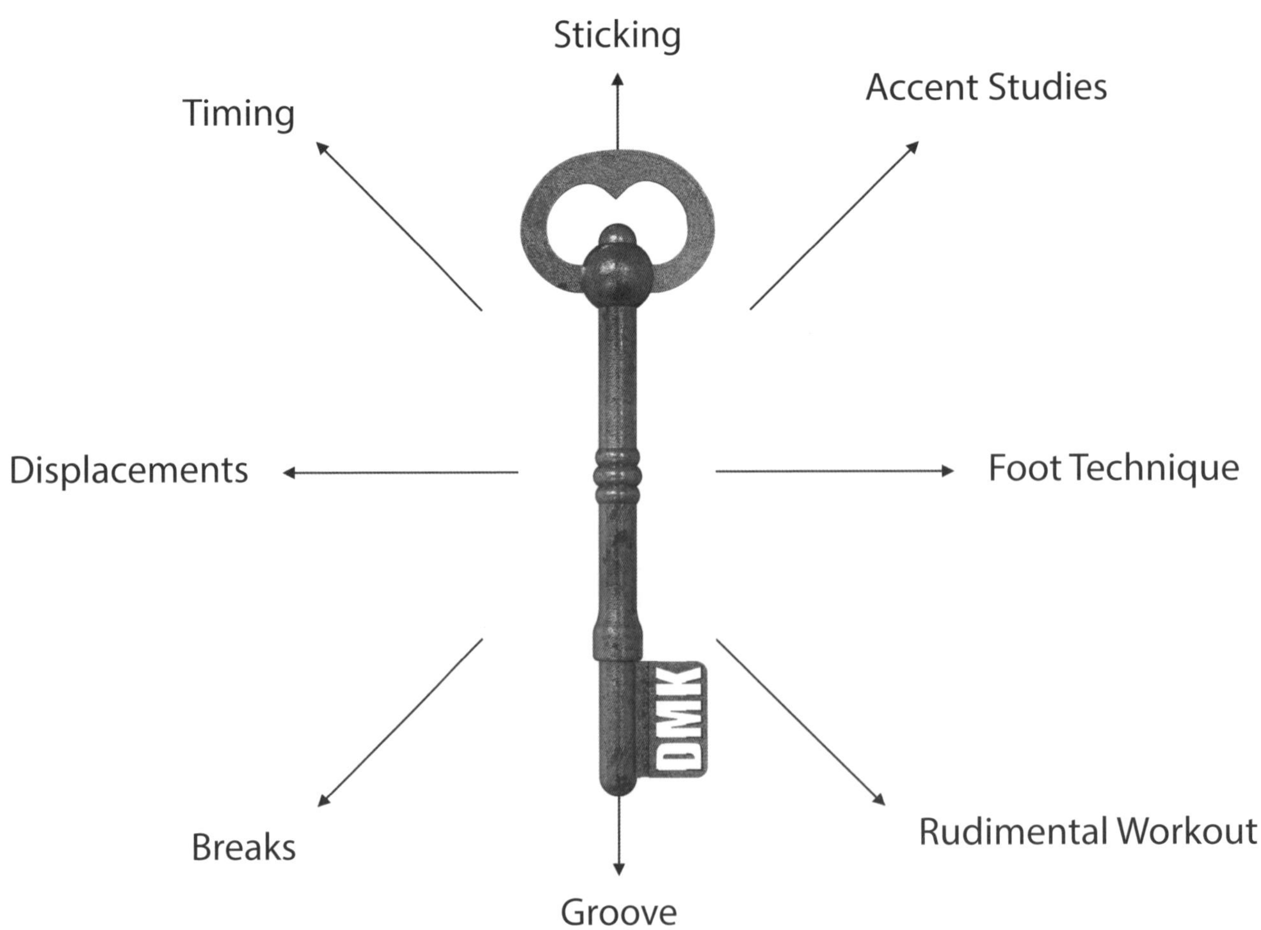

1st Phase Eighth Notes

At this point, abbreviations will be employed to enable the **Master Key** to be swiftly comprehended. You will find an exhaustive list of definitions for abbreviations below.

All combination possibilities are represented in the form of unfilled and filled note heads:

If, for example, all unfilled note heads are to be played with the right hand and all filled note heads with the left hand, this will be shown in the brief graphical representation as follows:

List of Abbreviations:

- **R** = Note is played with the **right hand**.
- **L** = Note is played with the **left hand**.
- **>** = Note should be **accentuated**.
- **flam** = Note is played with a **flam**.
- **x2** = Note value is **doubled**.
- **drag** = Note is played with a **drag**.
- **cym.** = Note is played on the **cymbal**.
- **SD** = Note is played on the **snare drum**.
- **BD** = Note is played on the **bass drum**.
- **TT** = Note is played on the **toms**.

Sticking

All **unfilled** note heads are played with the **right hand** and all **filled** note heads are played with the **left hand**.

Ex.:

Accent Studies

All **unfilled** note heads are played as an **unaccented** beat and all **filled** note heads are played as an **accented** beat.

Ex.:

Foot Technique

Exercise 1:

All **unfilled** note heads are played with the **right foot** and all **filled** note heads are played with the **left foot**. This exercise is suitable for playing on the hi-hat and bass drum and also with a double bass pedal.

Ex.:

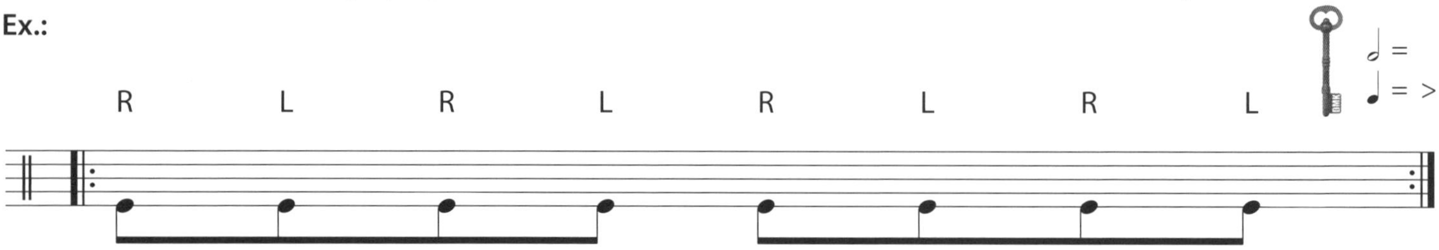

Exercise 2:

All **unfilled** note heads are played as **unaccented** beats and all **filled** note heads are played as an **accented** beats. I recommend playing the **unaccented** beats as **taps with heel down** and the **accented** beats as **contrary motion with heel up**.

Ex.:

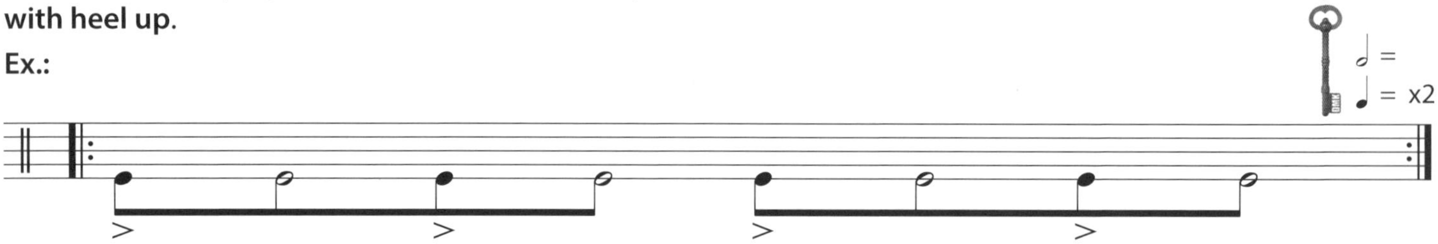

Rudimental Workout

Each exercise should be performed with one of the following stickings:

RLRL, LRLR, RRLL, LLRR, RLRR, LRLL, RLLR, LRRL, RLRL, LRLR.

Exercise 1:

A **flam** is played prior to each note with a **filled** note head.

Ex.:

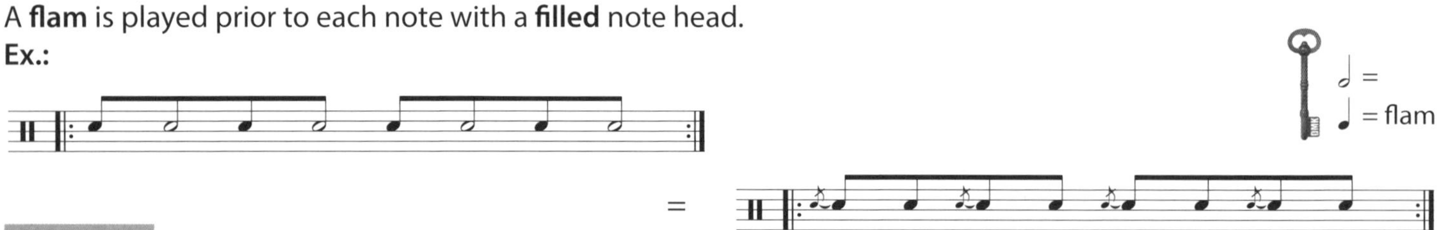

Exercise 2:

The value of each note with a **filled** note head is **doubled**.

Ex.:

Exercise 3:

The value of each note with a **filled** note head is **tripled**.

Ex.:

Exercise 4:

The value of each note with a **filled** note head is **quadrupled**.
Ex.:

=

Exercise 5:

A **drag** is played prior to each note with a **filled** note head.
Ex.:

=

Groove

Exercise 1: Rock / Pop

All **filled** note heads are played with the **right foot**.
The hands simultaneously play the **ostinato** as shown below:
Ex.:

+

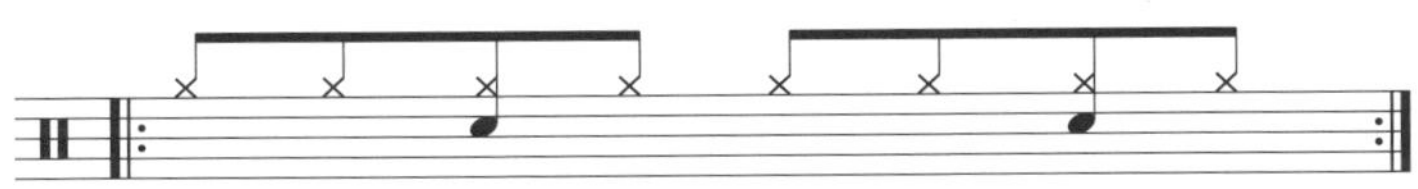

=

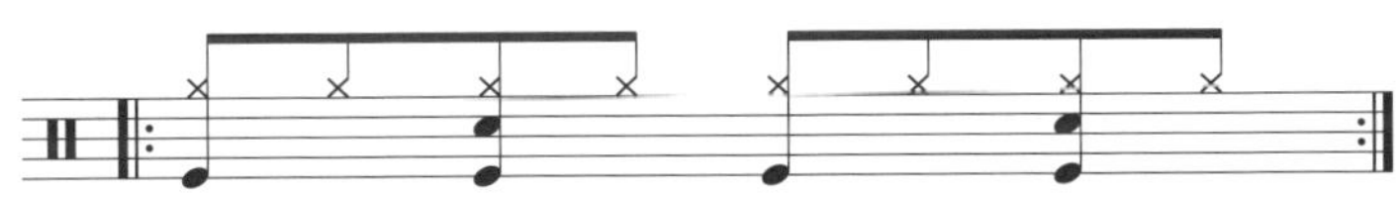

Exercise 2: Bossa Nova

All **filled** note heads are played with the **left hand** as a **rim click**.
The following **ostinato** is then added:
Ex.:

+

=

Exercise 3: Sticking Workout:

The same groove is repeated with different stickings. The stickings consist of the following patterns: **unfilled note head = right hand** and **filled note head = left hand.**

Ex.:

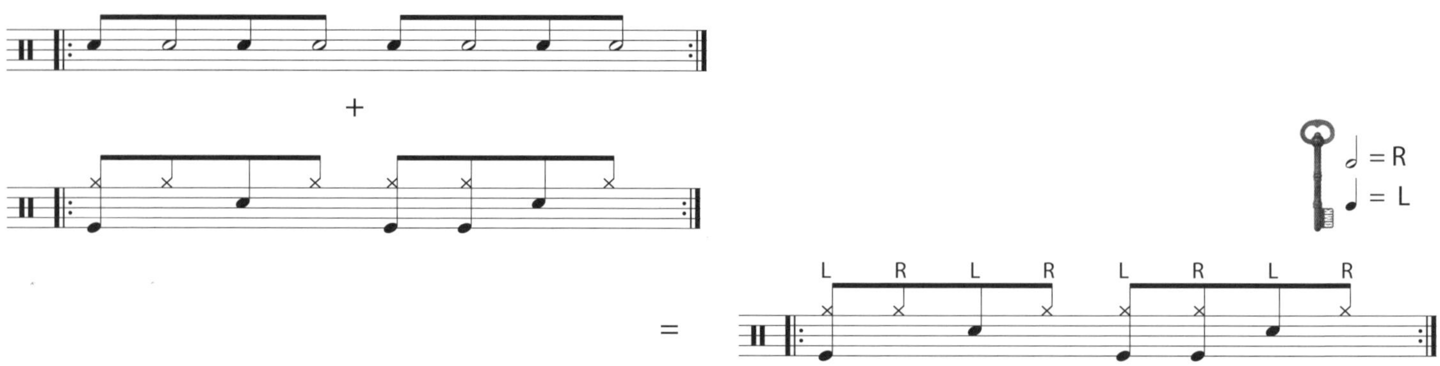

Breaks

Exercise 1:

All **filled** note heads are played with the **foot** and all **unfilled** note heads with the **hand**. The sticking and foot orchestration (hi-hat or bass drum) should be varied.

Ex.:

Exercise 2:

All **filled** note heads are played with a **cymbal and the bass drum** and all **unfilled** note heads as an **unaccented** beat on the **snare**. Different stickings can be utilized here (**RLRL, RRLL, etc.**).

Ex.:

Exercise 3:

All **filled** note heads are played on the **toms** and all **unfilled** note heads as an **unaccented** beat on the **snare**. Different stickings can be utilized here (**RLRL, RRLL, etc.**). Depending on which hand is used for the accented beat, the nearest tom is used respectively as orchestration (e.g. left hand = left rack tom and right hand = floor tom).

Ex.:

2nd Phase Eighth Notes

1

2

3

4

5

6

7

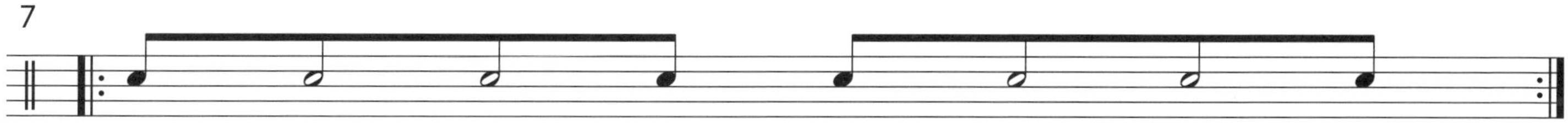

8

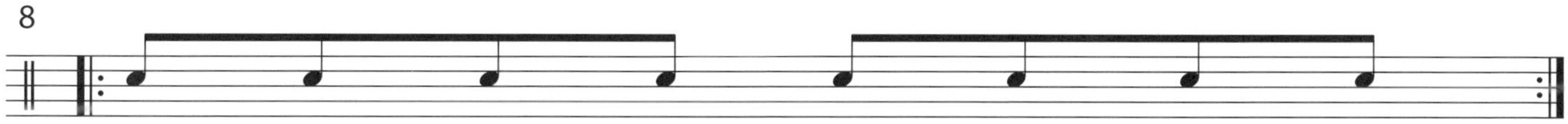

1st Phase Eighth-Note Triplets

Sticking

All **unfilled** note heads are played with the **right hand** and all **filled** note heads are played with the **left hand**.
Ex.:

Accent Studies

All **unfilled** note heads are played as an **unaccented** beat and all **filled** note heads are played as an **accented** beat.
Ex.:

Foot Technique

Exercise 1:

All **unfilled** note heads are played with the **right foot** and all **filled** note heads are played with the **left foot**.
This exercise is suitable for playing on the hi-hat and bass drum and also with a double bass pedal.
Ex.:

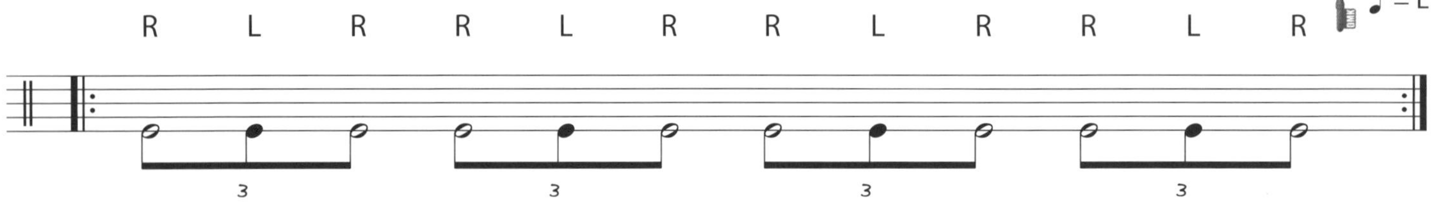

Exercise 2:

All **unfilled** note heads are played as **unaccented** beats and all **filled** note heads are played as **accented** beats.
I recommend playing the **unaccented** beats as **taps with heel down** and the **accented** beats as **contrary motion with heel up**.
Ex.:

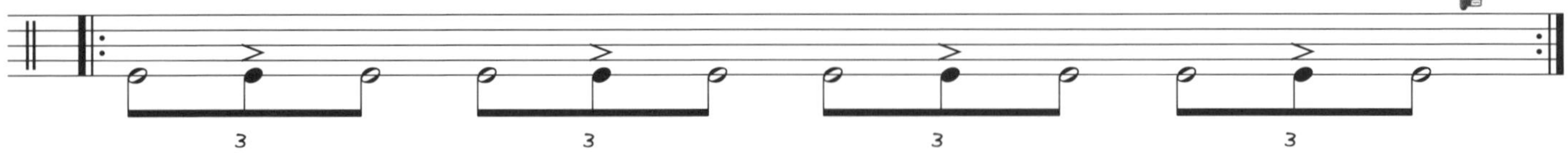

Rudimental Workout

Each exercise should be performed with one of the following stickings:
RLR, LRL, RRL, LLR, RLR, RLR, LRL, LRL, RLL, LRR, RLL, LRR.

Exercise 1:

A **flam** is played prior to each note with a **filled** note head.
Ex.:

Exercise 2:

The value of each note with a **filled** note head is **doubled**.
Ex.:

=

Exercise 3:

A **drag** is played prior to each note with a **filled** note head.
Ex.:

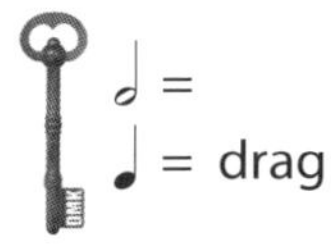

=

Groove

Exercise 1: Jazz Comping I

All **filled** note heads are played with the **snare drum**.
The right hand and the left foot simultaneously play the **ostinato** as shown below.
Ex.:

+

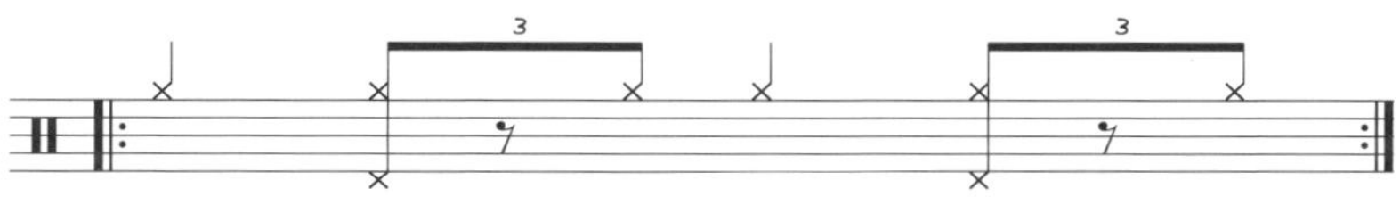

=

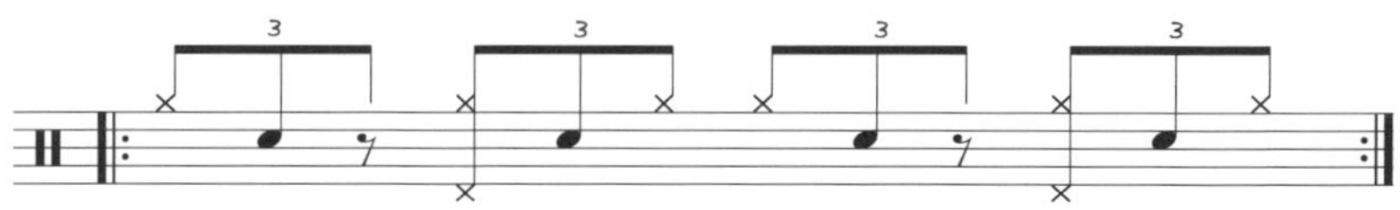

Exercise 2: Jazz Comping II

All **filled** note heads are played with the **bass drum**.
The right hand and the left foot simultaneously play the **ostinato** as shown below.
Ex.:

+

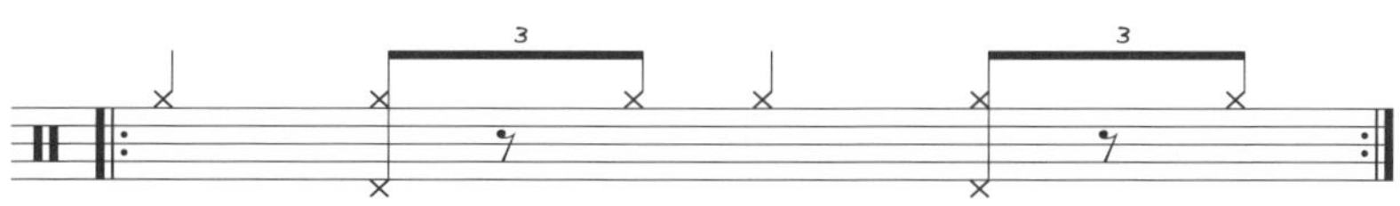

=

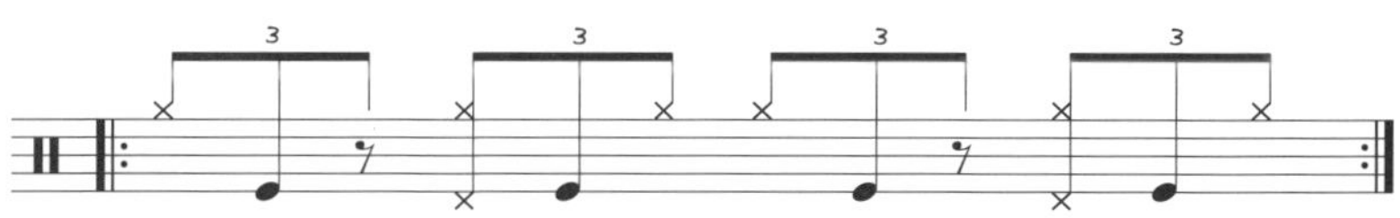

Exercise 3: Jazz Comping III

All **filled** note heads are played with the **hi-hat**.
The right hand plays the **ostinato** as shown below.
Ex.:

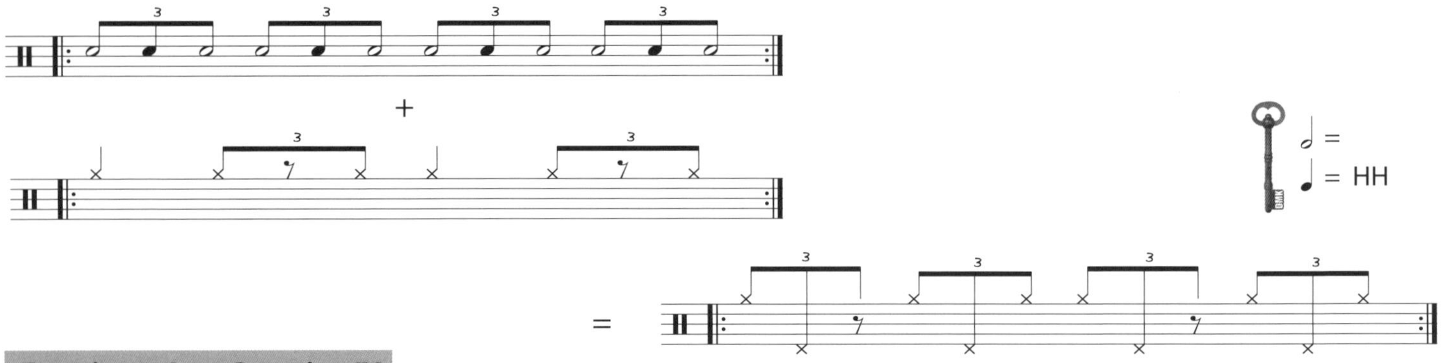

Exercise 4: Jazz Comping IV

All **filled** note heads are played with the **left foot and the right foot** alternating.
The right hand plays the **ostinato** as shown below:
Ex.:

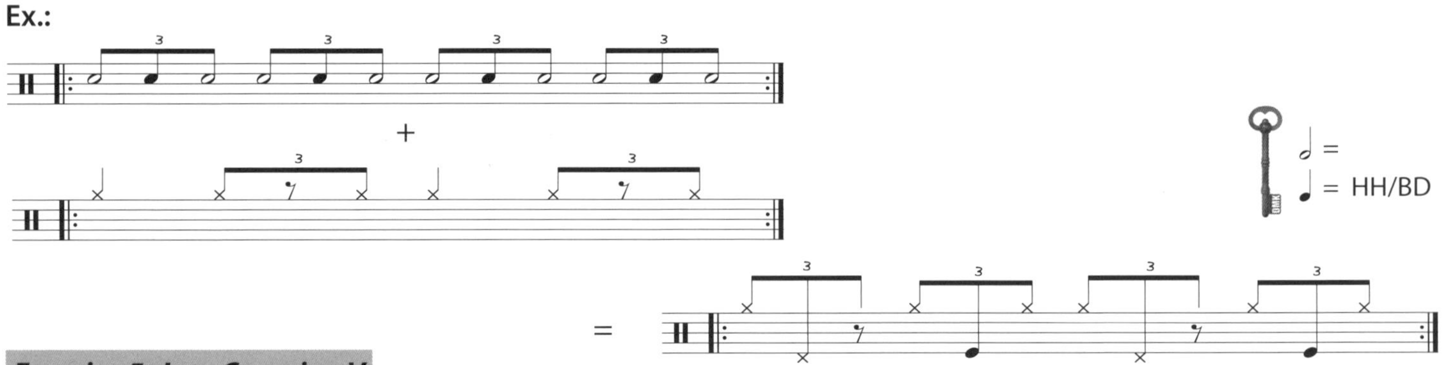

Exercise 5: Jazz Comping V

All **filled** note heads are played with the **snare drum and the bass drum** alternating.
The right hand and the left foot simultaneously play the **ostinato** as shown below.
Ex.:

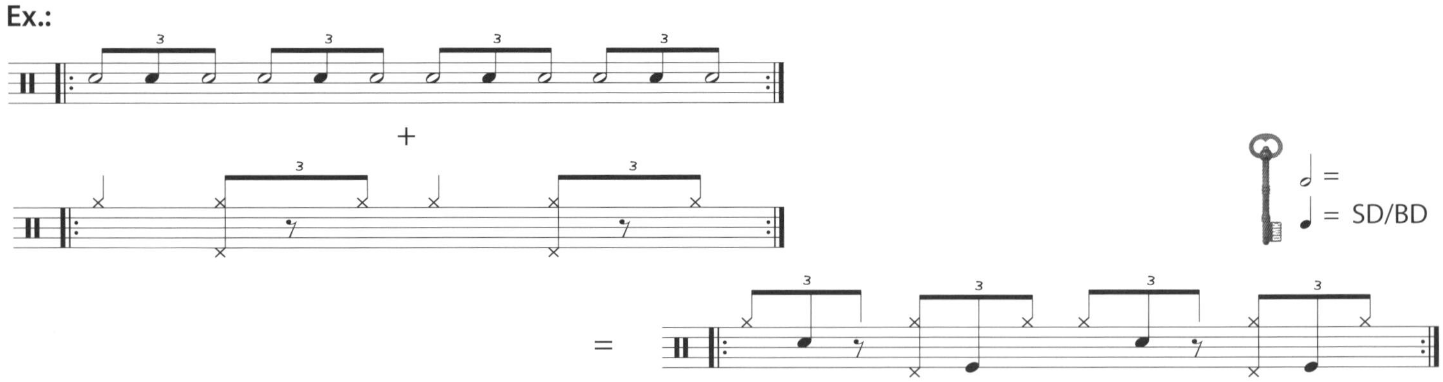

Exercise 6: Sticking Workout

The same groove is repeated with **different stickings.** The stickings consist of the following patterns:
unfilled note head = right hand and **filled note head = left hand**.
Ex.:

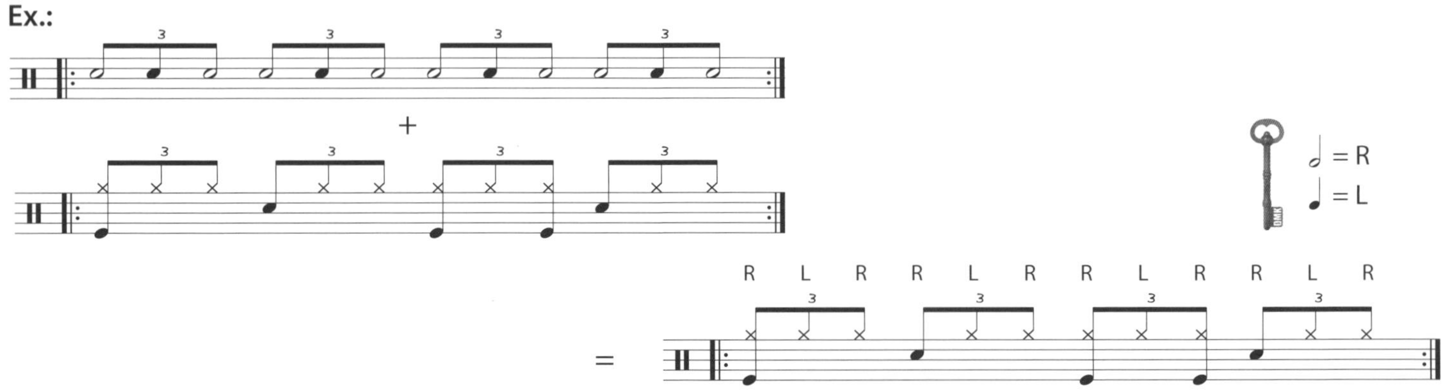

Breaks

Exercise 1:

All **filled** note heads are played with the **foot** and all **unfilled** note heads with the **hand**. The sticking and foot orchestration (hi-hat or bass drum) should be varied.

Ex.:

=

Exercise 2:

All **filled** note heads are played with a **cymbal and the bass drum** and all **unfilled** note heads as an **unaccented** beat on the **snare**. Different stickings can be utilized here (**RLR, RLL, etc.**).

Ex.:

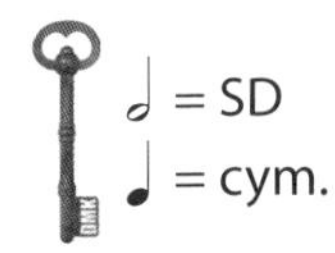

=

Exercise 3:

All **filled** note heads are played on the **toms** and all **unfilled** note heads as an **unaccented** beat on the **snare**. Different stickings can be utilized here. Depending on which hand is used for the accented beat, the nearest tom is used respectively as orchestration (e.g. left hand = left rack tom and right hand = floor tom).

Ex.:

=

2nd Phase Eighth-Note Triplets

1

2

3

4

5

6

7

8

1st Phase Sixteenth Notes

Sticking

All **unfilled** note heads are played with the **right hand** and all **filled** note heads are played with the **left hand**.
Ex.:

Accent Studies

All **unfilled** note heads are played as an **unaccented** beat and all **filled** note heads are played as an **accented** beat.
Ex.:

Foot Technique

Exercise 1:

All **unfilled** note heads are played with the **right foot** and all **filled** note heads are played with the **left foot**.
This exercise is suitable for playing on the hi-hat and bass drum and also with a double bass pedal.
Ex.:

Exercise 2:

All **unfilled** note heads are played as **unaccented** beats and all **filled** note heads are played as **accented** beats.
I recommend playing the **unaccented** beats as **taps with heel down** and the **accented** beats as **contrary motion with heel up**.
Ex.:

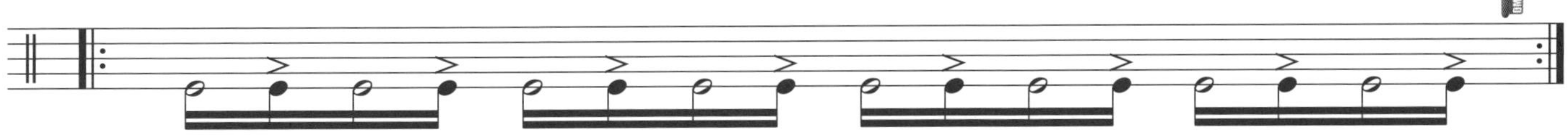

Rudimental Workout

Each exercise should be performed with one of the following stickings: **RLRL, LRLR, RRLL, RLRR, LRLL, etc.**

Exercise 1:

A **flam** is played prior to each note with a **filled** note head.

Exercise 2:

The value of each note with a **filled** note head is **doubled**.
Ex.:

Exercise 3:

A **drag** is played prior to each note with a **filled** note head.
Ex.:

Groove

Exercise 1: Funk / Pop I

All **filled** note heads are played with the **foot**.
The hands simultaneously play the **ostinato** as shown below: (**RLRL, RRLL, RRRR, etc.**).
Ex.:

+

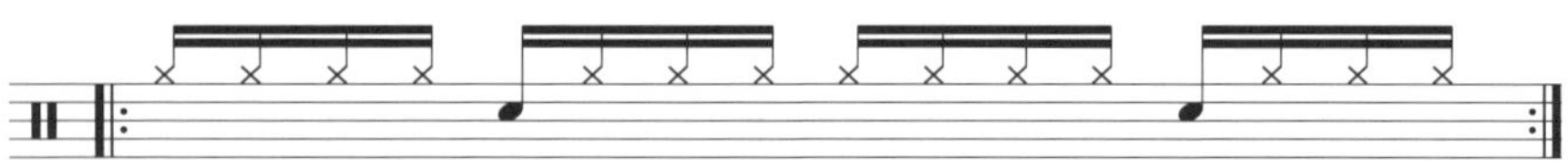

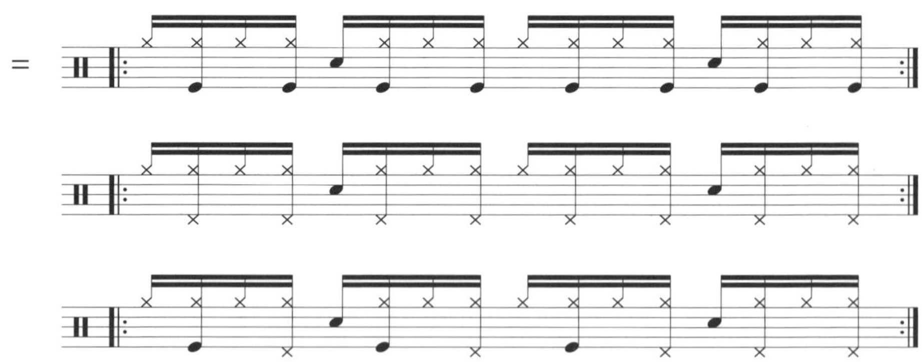

Exercise 2: Funk / Pop II

All **filled** note heads are played with the **left hand** as a **rim click**.
The following **ostinato** is then added:
Ex.:

+

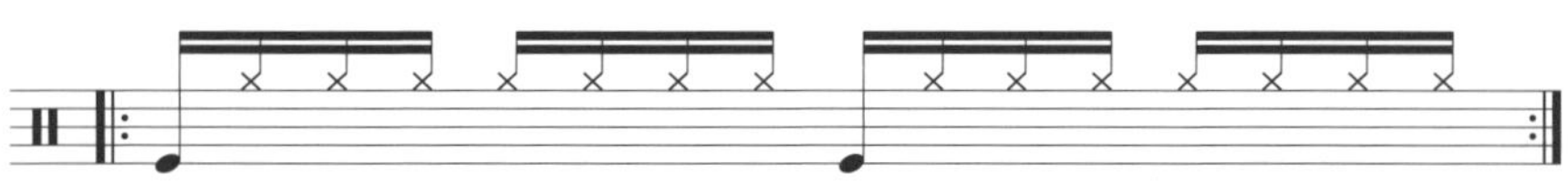

Exercise 3: Sticking Workout

The same groove is repeated with different stickings. The stickings consist of the following patterns:
unfilled note head = right hand and **filled note head = left hand**.

Ex.:

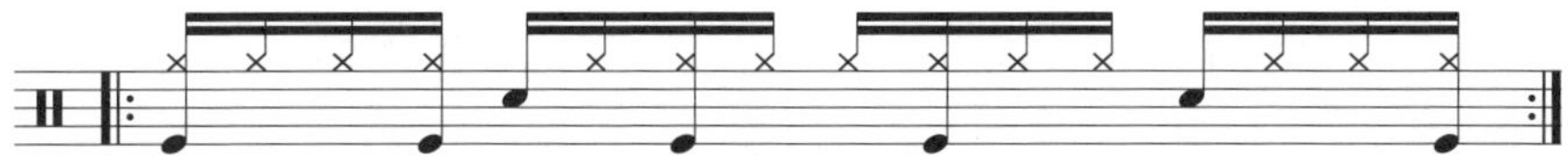

Breaks

Exercise 1:

All **filled** note heads are played with the **foot** and all **unfilled** note heads with the **hand**. The sticking and foot orchestration (hi-hat or bass drum) should be varied.

Ex.:

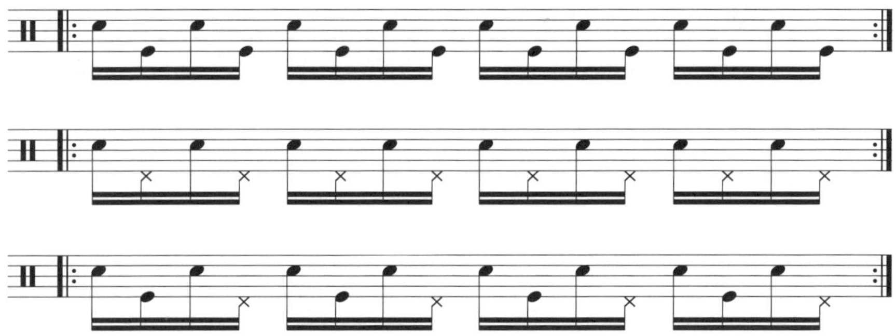

Exercise 2:

All **filled** note heads are played with a **cymbal and the bass drum** and all **unfilled** note heads as **unaccented** beats on the **snare**. Different stickings can be utilized here (**RLRL, RRLL, etc.**).

Ex.:

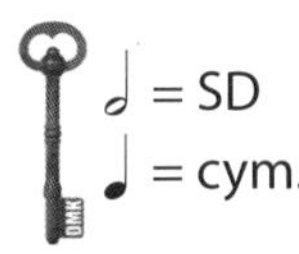

Exercise 3:

All **filled** note heads are played on the **toms** and all **unfilled** note heads as **unaccented** beats on the **snare**. Different stickings can be utilized here (**RLRL, RRLL, etc.**). Depending on which hand is used for the accented beat, the nearest tom is used respectively as orchestration (e.g. left hand = left rack tom and right hand = floor tom).

Ex.:

2nd Phase Sixteenth Notes

1

2

3

4

5

6

7

8

9

10

11

12

13

14

15

16

1st Phase Quintuplets

Sticking

All **unfilled** note heads are played with the **right hand** and all **filled** note heads are played with the **left hand**.
Ex.:

Accent Studies

All **unfilled** note heads are played as an **unaccented** beat and all **filled** note heads are played as an **accented** beat.
Ex.:

Foot Technique

Exercise 1:

All **unfilled** note heads are played with the **right foot** and all **filled** note heads are played with the **left foot**.
This exercise is suitable for playing on the hi-hat and bass drum and also with a double bass pedal.
Ex.:

Exercise 2:

All **unfilled** note heads are played as **unaccented** beats and all **filled** note heads are played as **accented** beats.
I recommend playing the **unaccented** beats as **taps with heel down** and the **accented** beats as **contrary motion with heel up**.
Ex.:

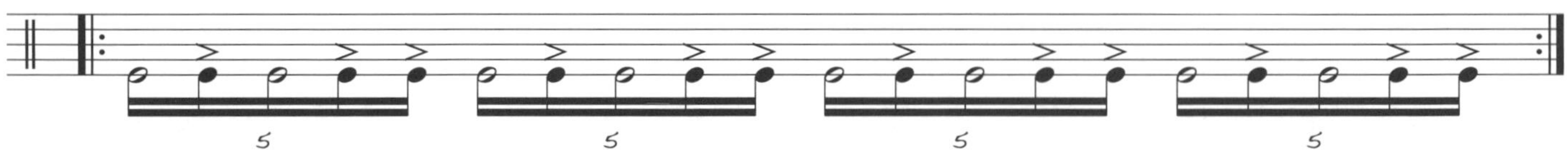

Rudimental Workout

Each exercise should be performed with one of the following stickings: **RLRLL, LLRLR, RRLLL, RLRRL, etc.**

Exercise 1:

A **flam** is played prior to each note with a **filled** note head.
Ex.:

Exercise 2:

The value of each note with a **filled** note head is **doubled**.

Ex.:

Exercise 3:

A **drag** is played prior to each note with a **filled** note head.

Ex.:

Groove

Exercise 1:

All **filled** note heads are played with the foot. The hands simultaneously play the **ostinato** as shown below. Each exercise should be performed with varied stickings (**RLRLL, RRLLL, etc.**).

Ex.:

Exercise 2:

All **filled** note heads are played with the **left hand** as a **rim click**.
The following **ostinato** is then added:

Ex.:

Exercise 3: Sticking Workout

The same groove is repeated with different stickings. The stickings consist of the following patterns:
unfilled note head = right hand and **filled note head = left hand.**

Ex.:

+

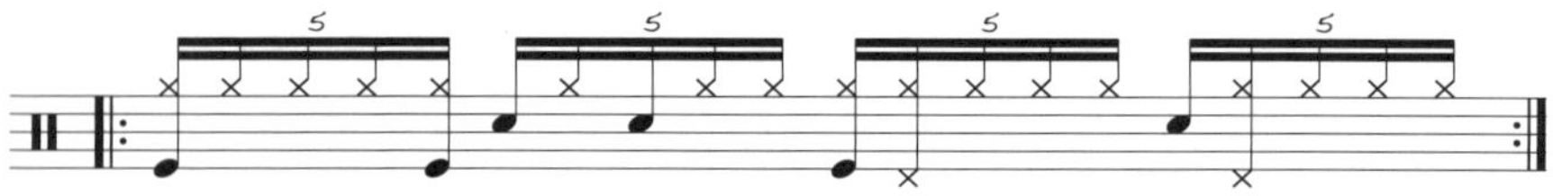

=

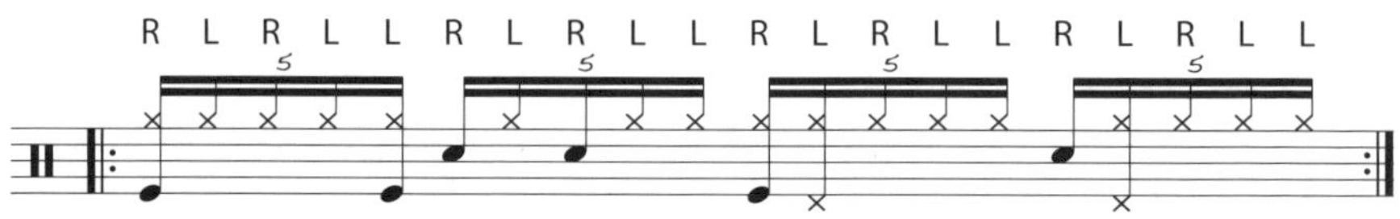

Breaks

Exercise 1:

All **filled** note heads are played with the **foot** and all **unfilled** note heads with the **hand**.
The sticking and foot orchestration (hi-hat or bass drum) should be varied.

Ex.:

=

Exercise 2:

All **filled** note heads are played with a **cymbal and the bass drum** and all **unfilled** note heads as **unaccented** beats on the **snare**. Different stickings can be utilized here (**RLRLL, RRLLL, etc.**).

Ex.:

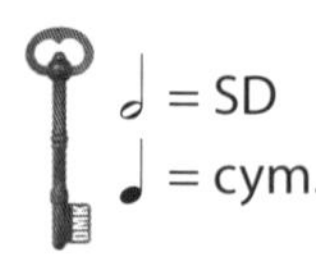

=

Exercise 3:

All **filled** note heads are played on the **toms** and all **unfilled** note heads as **unaccented** beats on the **snare**. Different stickings can be utilized here. Depending on which hand is used for the accented beat, the nearest tom is used respectively as orchestration (e.g. left hand = left rack tom and right hand = floor tom).

Ex.:

=

2nd Phase Quintuplets

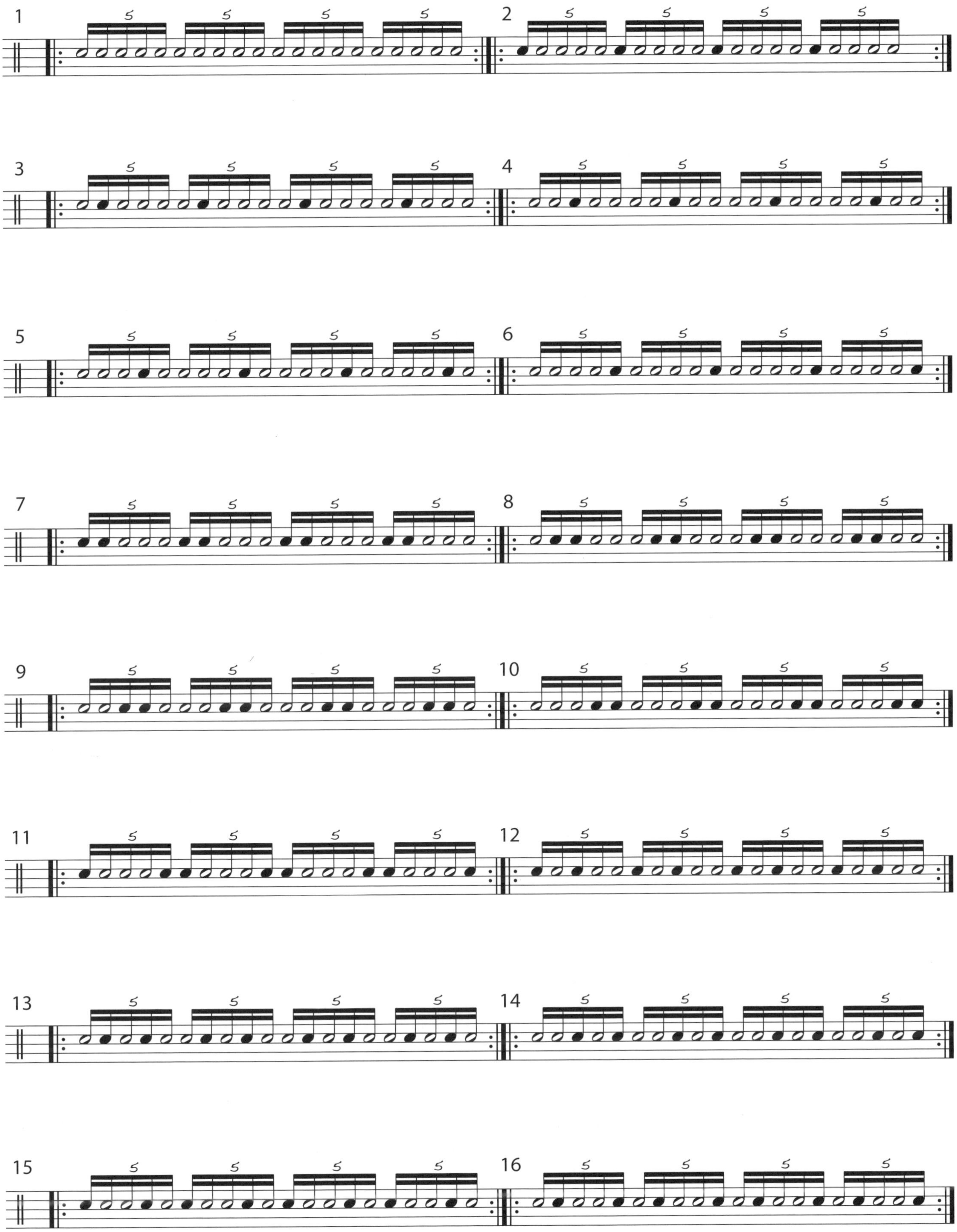

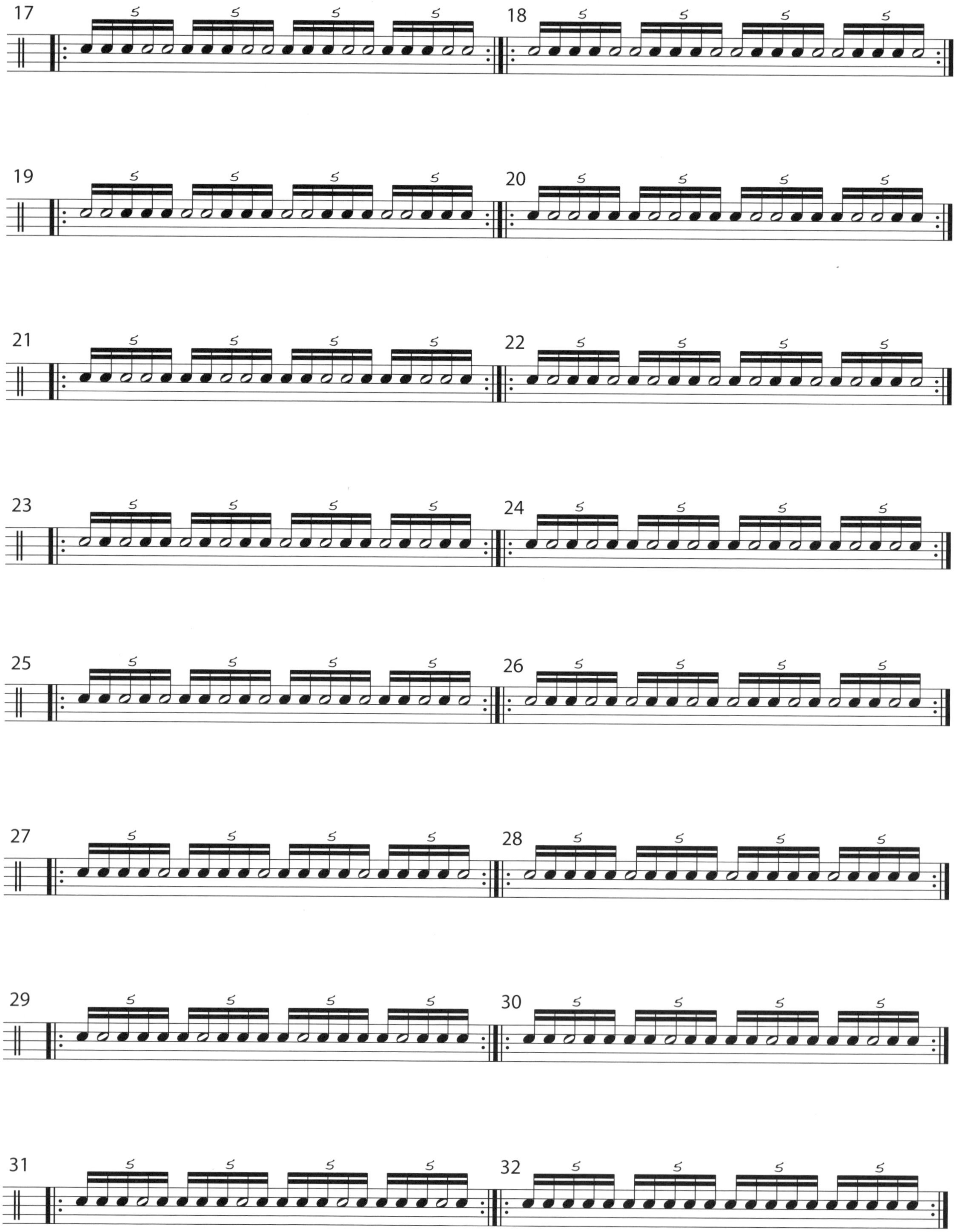
17
18
19
20
21
22
23
24
25
26
27
28
29
30
31
32

1st Phase Sixteenth-Note Triplets/Sextuplets

Sticking

All **unfilled** note heads are played with the **right hand** and all **filled** note heads are played with the **left hand**.

Ex.:

Accent Studies

All **unfilled** note heads are played as an **unaccented** beat and all **filled** note heads are played as an **accented** beat.

Ex.:

Foot Technique

Exercise 1:

All **unfilled** note heads are played with the **right foot** and all **filled** note heads are played with the **left foot**.
This exercise is suitable for playing on the hi-hat and bass drum and also with a double bass pedal.

Ex.:

Exercise 2:

All **unfilled** note heads are played as **unaccented** beats and all **filled** note heads are played as **accented** beats.
I recommend playing the **unaccented** beats as **taps with heel down** and the **accented** beats as **contrary motion with heel up**.

Ex.:

Each exercise should be performed with one of the following stickings: **RLR, LRL, etc.**

Exercise 1:

A **flam** is played prior to each note with a **filled** note head.

Ex.:

=

Exercise 2:

The value of each note with a **filled** note head is **doubled**.

Ex.:

=

Exercise 3:

A **drag** is played prior to each note with a **filled** note head.

Ex.:

=

Groove

Exercise 1: Shuffle

All **filled** note heads are played with the **foot**.
The hands simultaneously play the **ostinato** as shown below (**RLR, LRL, etc.**).

Ex.:

+

=

Exercise 1: Reggae

All **filled** note heads are played with the **left hand** as a **rim click**.
The following **ostinato** is then added:

Ex.:

+

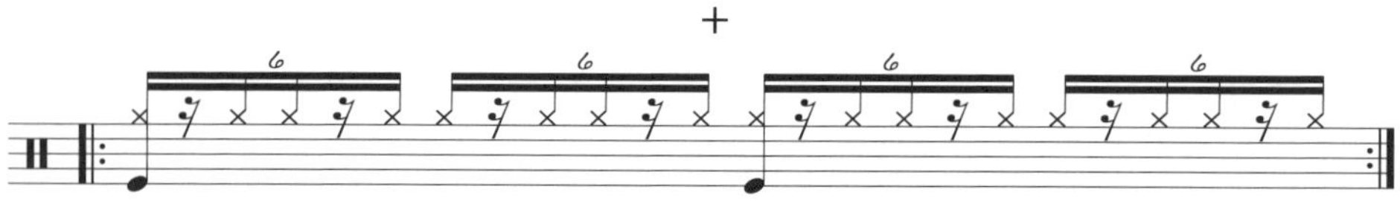

=

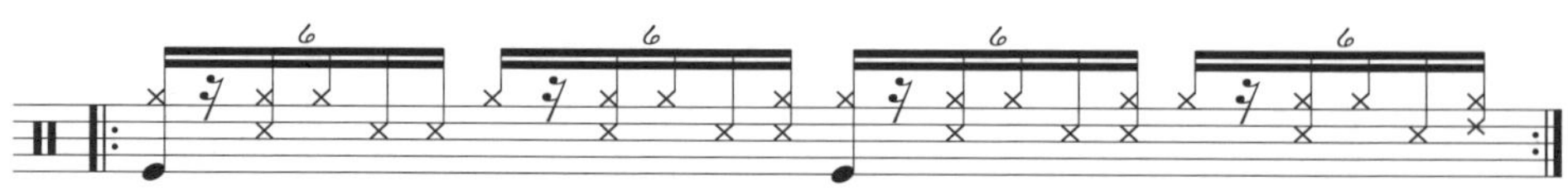

Exercise 3: Sticking Workout

The same groove is repeated with different stickings. The stickings consist of the following patterns:
unfilled note head = right hand and **filled note head = left hand**.

Ex.:

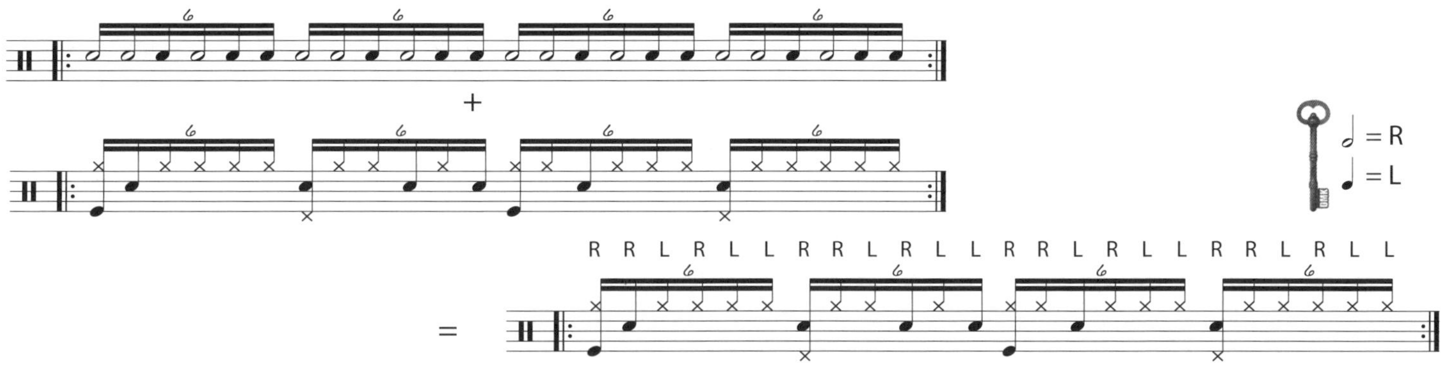

Breaks

Exercise 1:

All **filled** note heads are played with the **foot** and all **unfilled** note heads with the **hand**. The sticking and foot orchestration (hi-hat or bass drum) should be varied.

Ex.:

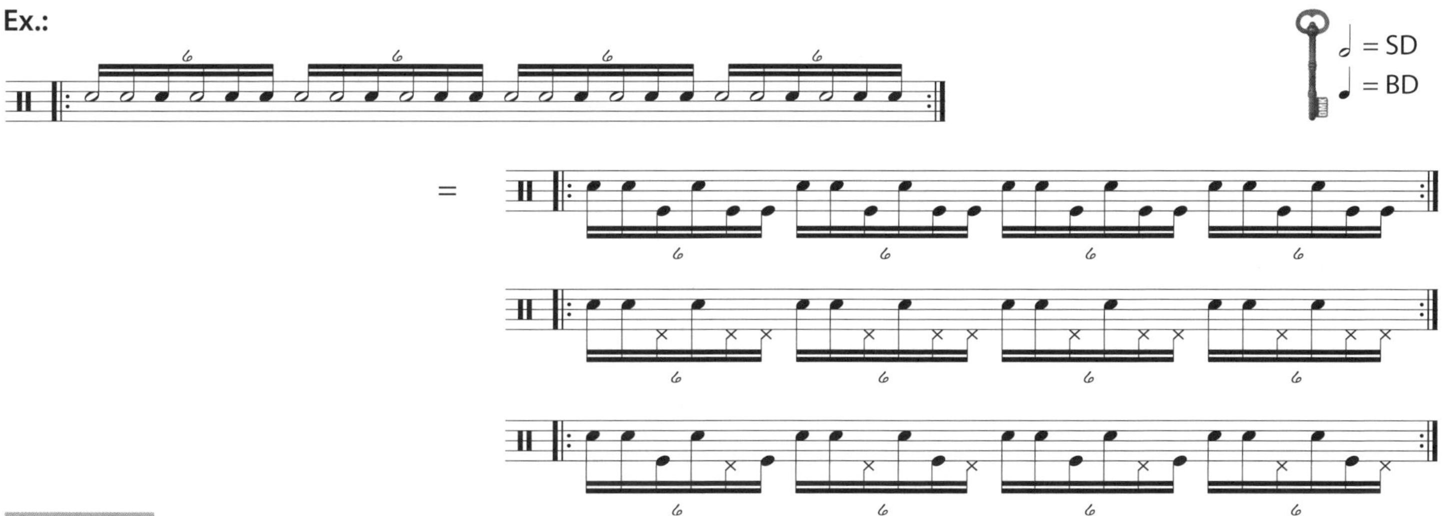

Exercise 2:

All **filled** note heads are played with a **cymbal and the bass drum** and all **unfilled** note heads as **unaccented** beats on the **snare**. Different stickings can be utilized here (**RLR, LRL, etc.**).

Ex.:

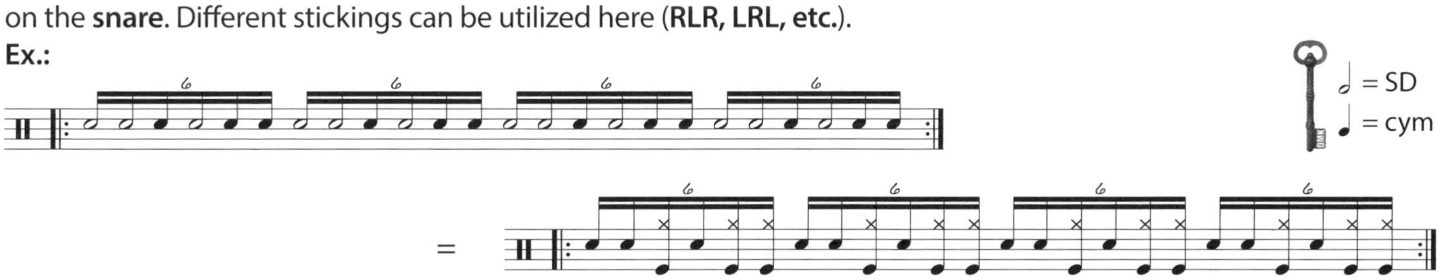

Exercise 3:

All **filled** note heads are played on the **toms** and all **unfilled** note heads as **unaccented** beats on the **snare**. Different stickings can be utilized here (**RLRL, RRLL, etc.**). Depending on which hand is used for the accented beat, the nearest tom is used respectively as orchestration (e.g. left hand = left rack tom and right hand = floor tom).

Ex.:

2nd Phase Sixteenth-Note Triplets/Sextuplets

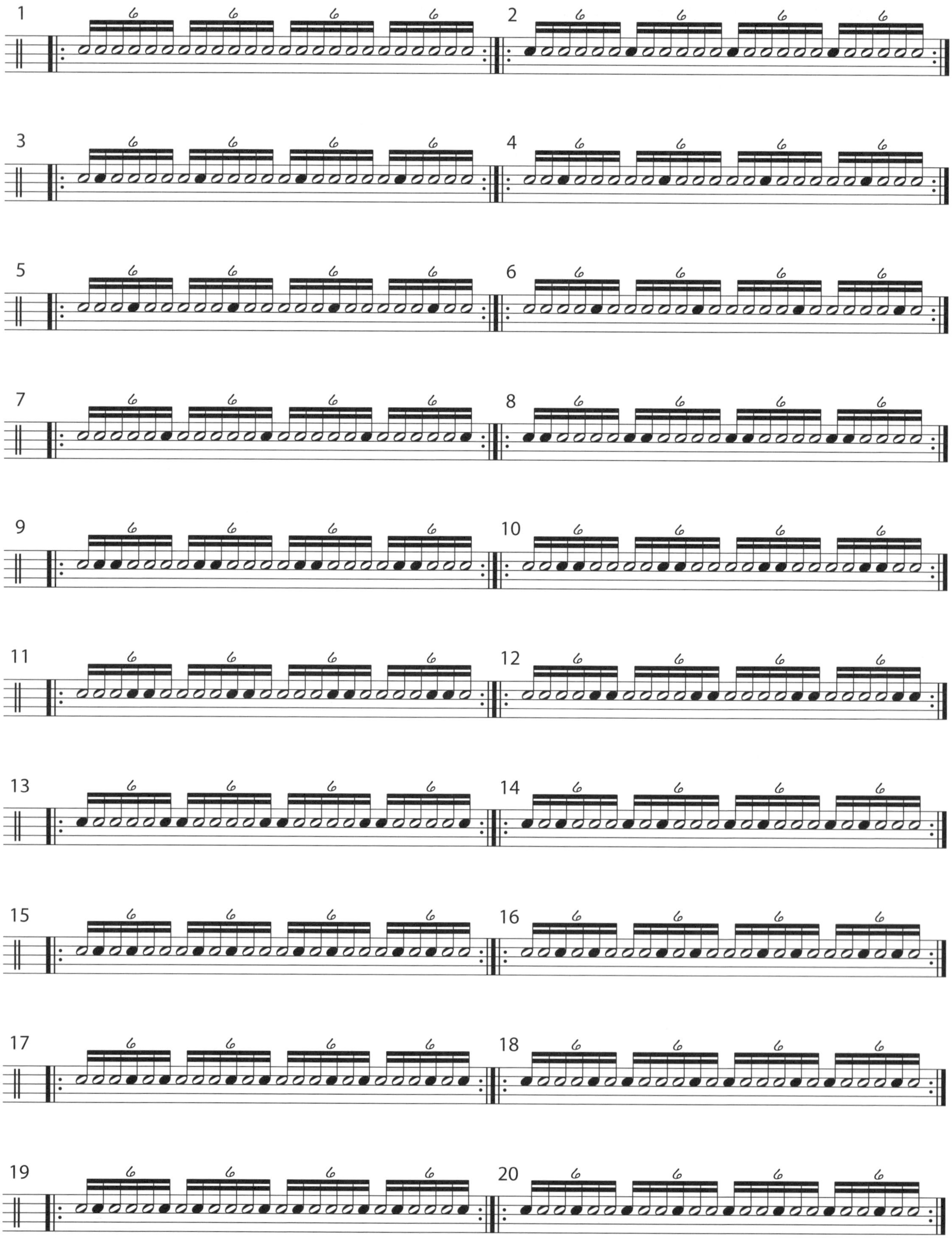

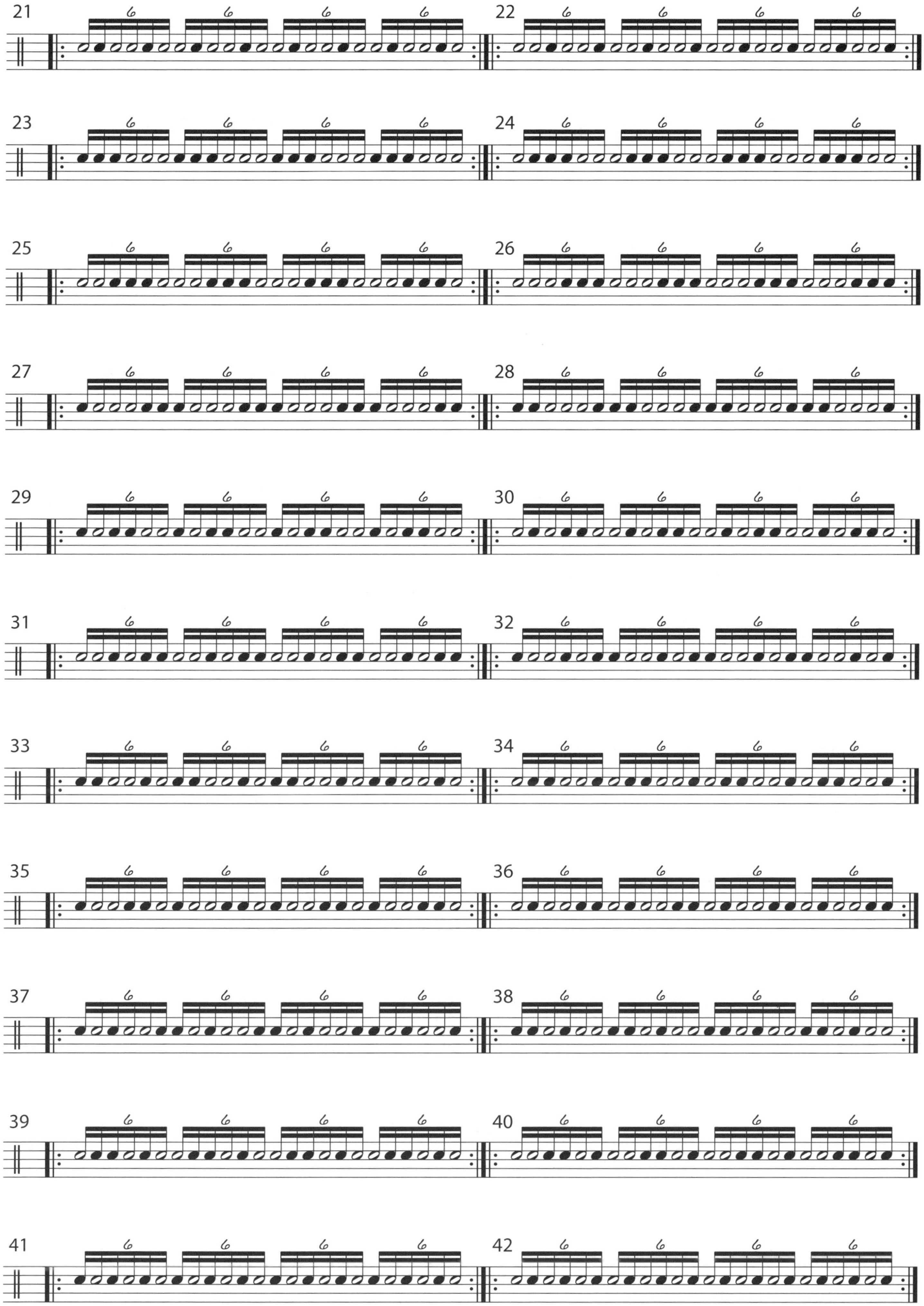
21
22
23
24
25
26
27
28
29
30
31
32
33
34
35
36
37
38
39
40
41
42

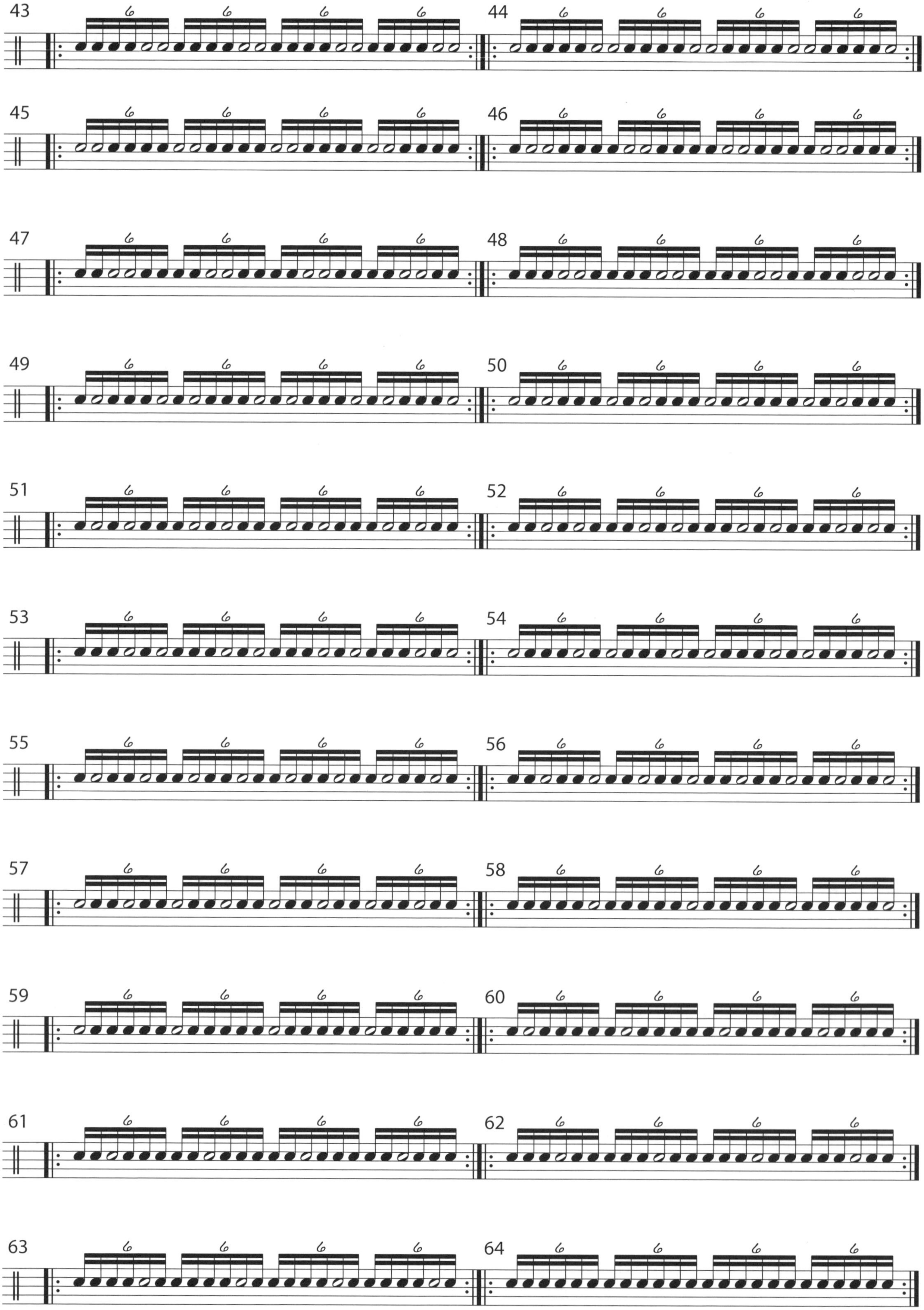
43
44
45
46
47
48
49
50
51
52
53
54
55
56
57
58
59
60
61
62
63
64

1st Phase Septuplets

Sticking

All **unfilled** note heads are played with the **right hand** and all **filled** note heads are played with the **left hand**.
Ex.:

Accent Studies

All **unfilled** note heads are played as an **unaccented** beat and all **filled** note heads are played as an **accented** beat.
Ex.:

Foot Technique

Exercise 1:

All **unfilled** note heads are played with the **right foot** and all **filled** note heads are played with the **left foot**.
This exercise is suitable for playing on the hi-hat and bass drum and also with a double bass pedal.
Ex.:

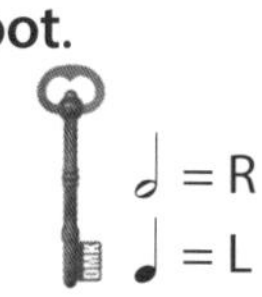

Exercise 2:

All **unfilled** note heads are played as **unaccented** beats and all **filled** note heads are played as **accented** beats.
I recommend playing the **unaccented** beats as **taps with heel down** and the **accented** beats as **contrary motion with heel up**.
Ex.:

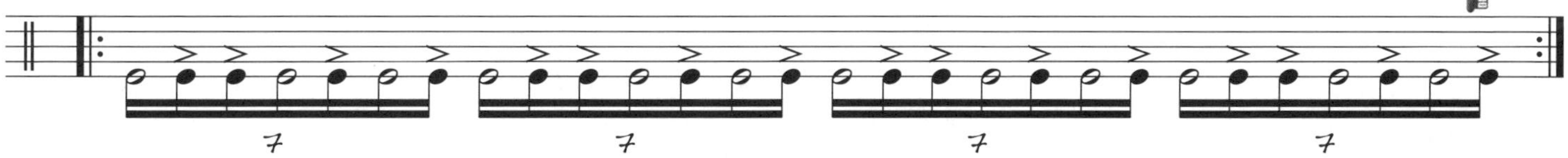

Rudimental Workout

Each exercise should be performed with the following sticking: **RLRRLRL**, etc.

Exercise 1:

A **flam** is played prior to each note with a **filled** note head.
Ex.:

=

Exercise 2:

The value of each note with a **filled** note head is **doubled**.

Ex.:

Exercise 3:

A **drag** is played prior to each note with a **filled** note head.

Ex.:

Groove

Exercise 1:

All **filled** note heads are played with the **foot**.

The hands simultaneously play the **ostinato** as shown below: (**RLRR, LRL, etc.**).

Ex.:

+

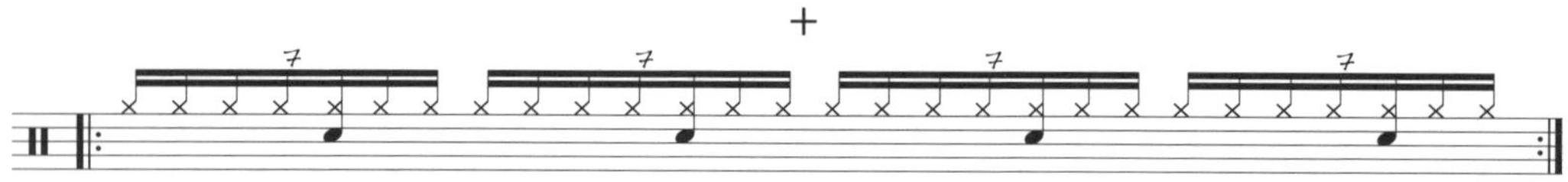

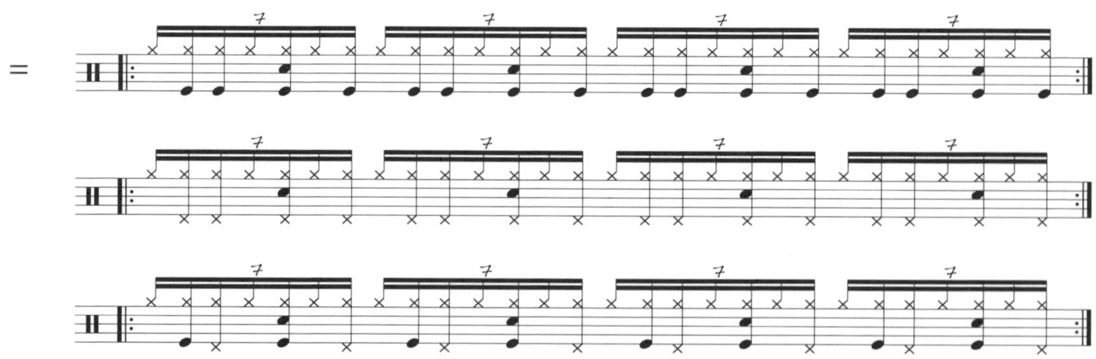

Exercise 2:

All **filled** note heads are played with the **left hand** as a **rim click**.

Ex.:

The following **ostinato** is then added: +

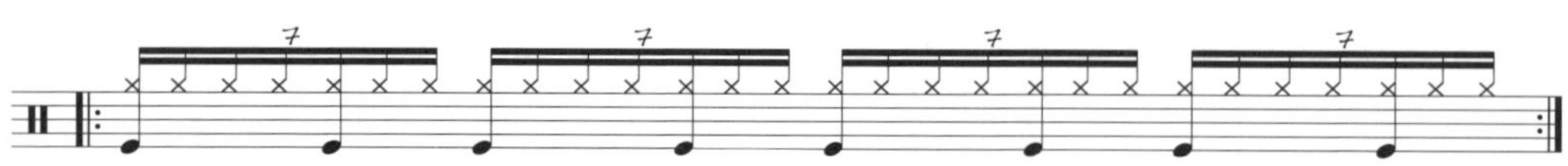

Exercise 3: Sticking Workout

The same groove is repeated with different stickings. The stickings consist of the following patterns:
unfilled note head = right hand and **filled note head = left hand**.

Ex.:

Breaks

Exercise 1:

All **filled** note heads are played with the **foot** and all **unfilled** note heads with the **hand**.
The sticking and foot orchestration (hi-hat or bass drum) should be varied.

Ex.:

Exercise 2:

All **filled** note heads are played with a **cymbal and the bass drum** and all **unfilled** note heads as **unaccented** beats on the **snare**. Use the following sticking: **RLRRLRL**.

Ex.:

Exercise 3:

All **filled** note heads are played on the **toms** and all **unfilled** note heads as **unaccented** beats on the **snare**. Different stickings can be utilized here (**RLRL, RRLL, etc.**). Depending on which hand is used for the accented beat, the nearest tom is used respectively as orchestration (e.g. left hand = left rack tom and right hand = floor tom).

Ex.:

2nd Phase Septuplets

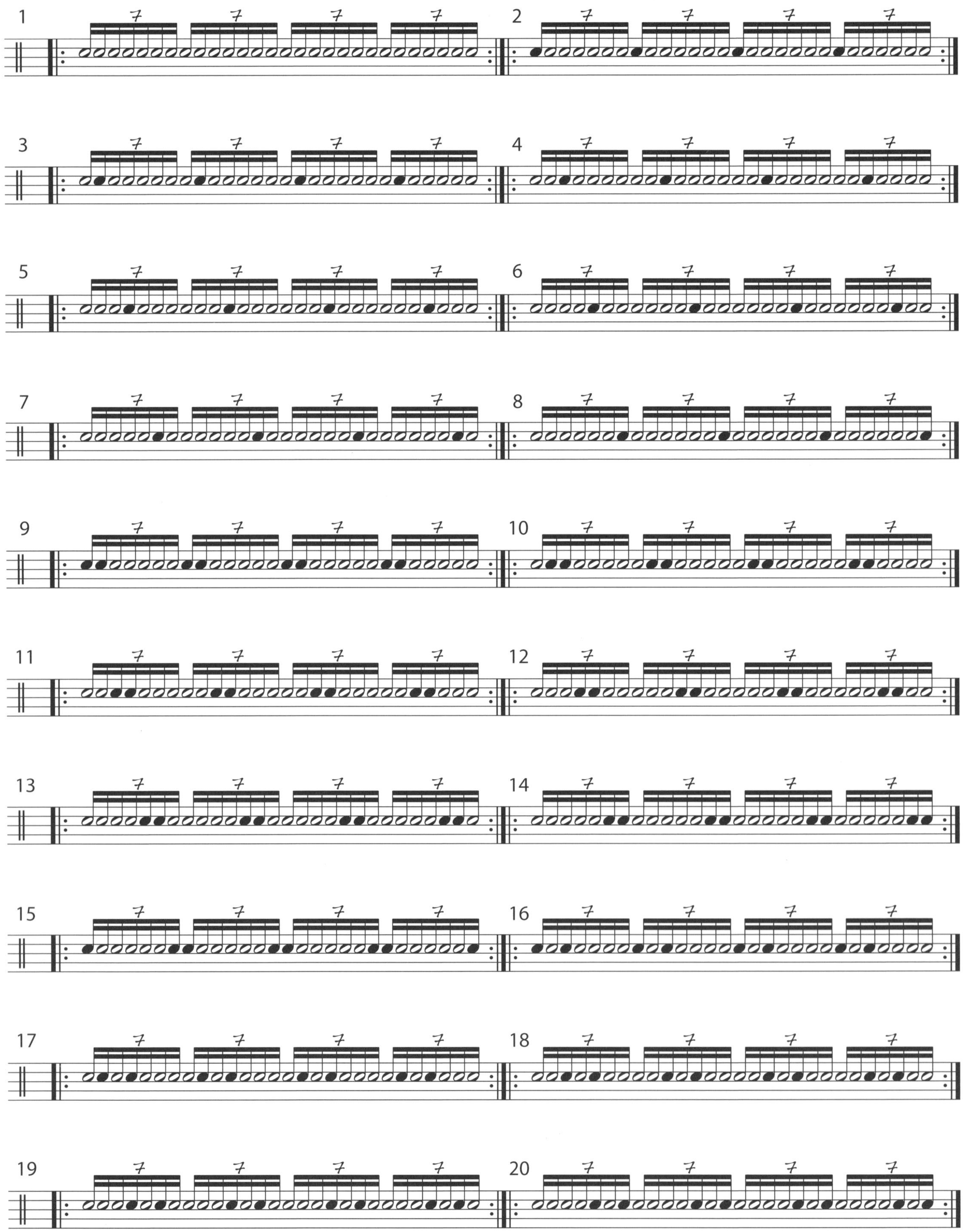

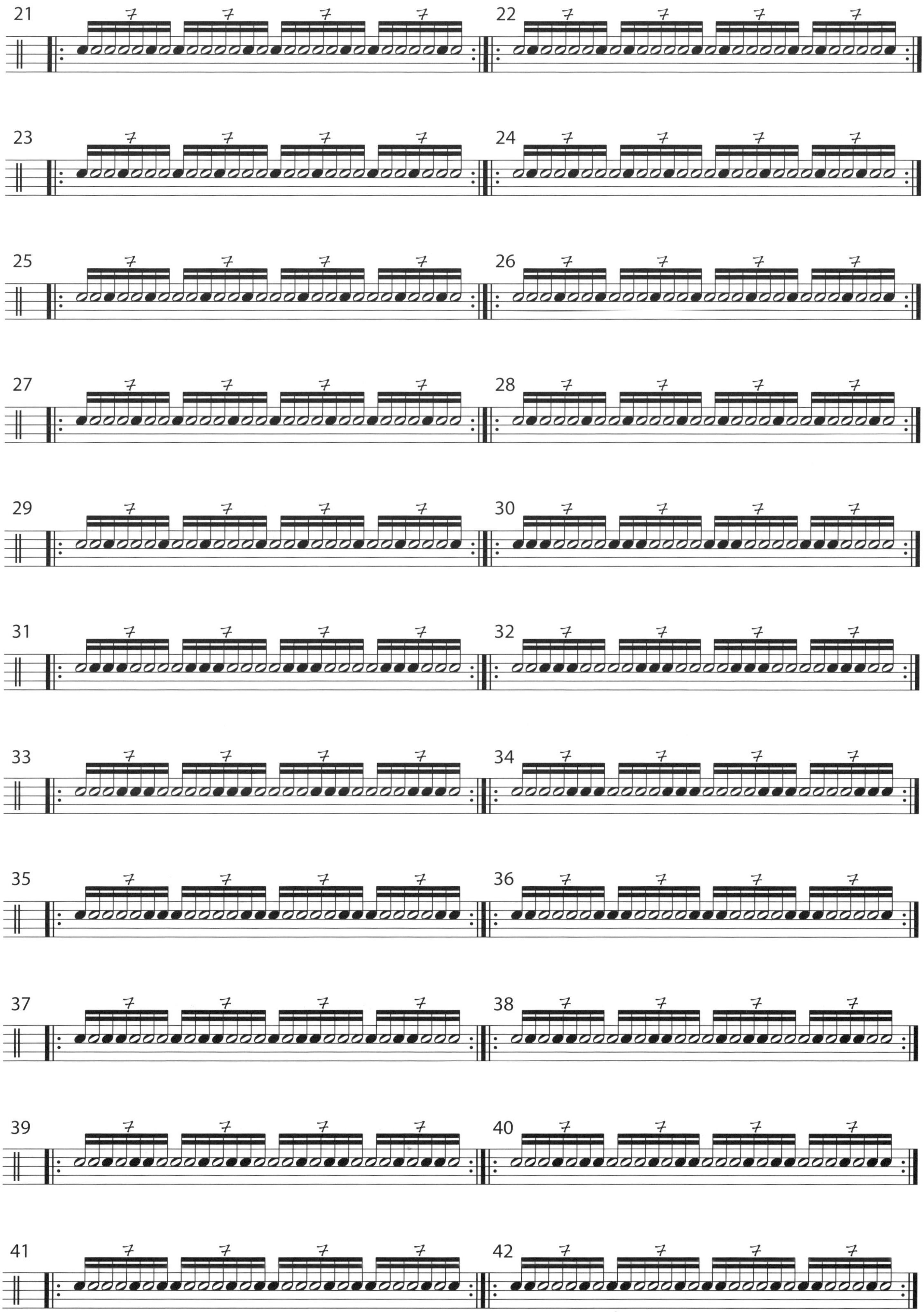
21
22
23
24
25
26
27
28
29
30
31
32
33
34
35
36
37
38
39
40
41
42

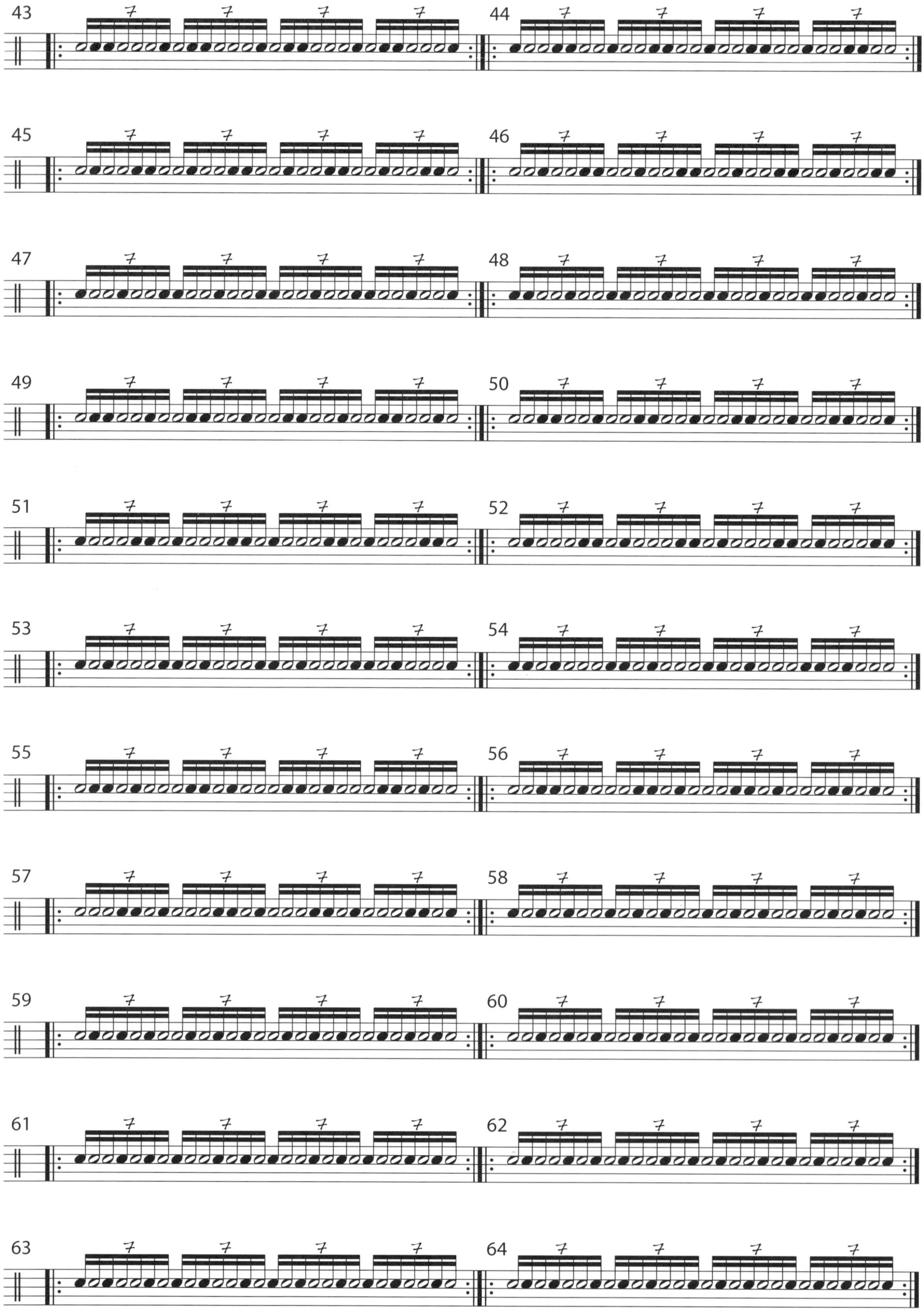
43
44
45
46
47
48
49
50
51
52
53
54
55
56
57
58
59
60
61
62
63
64

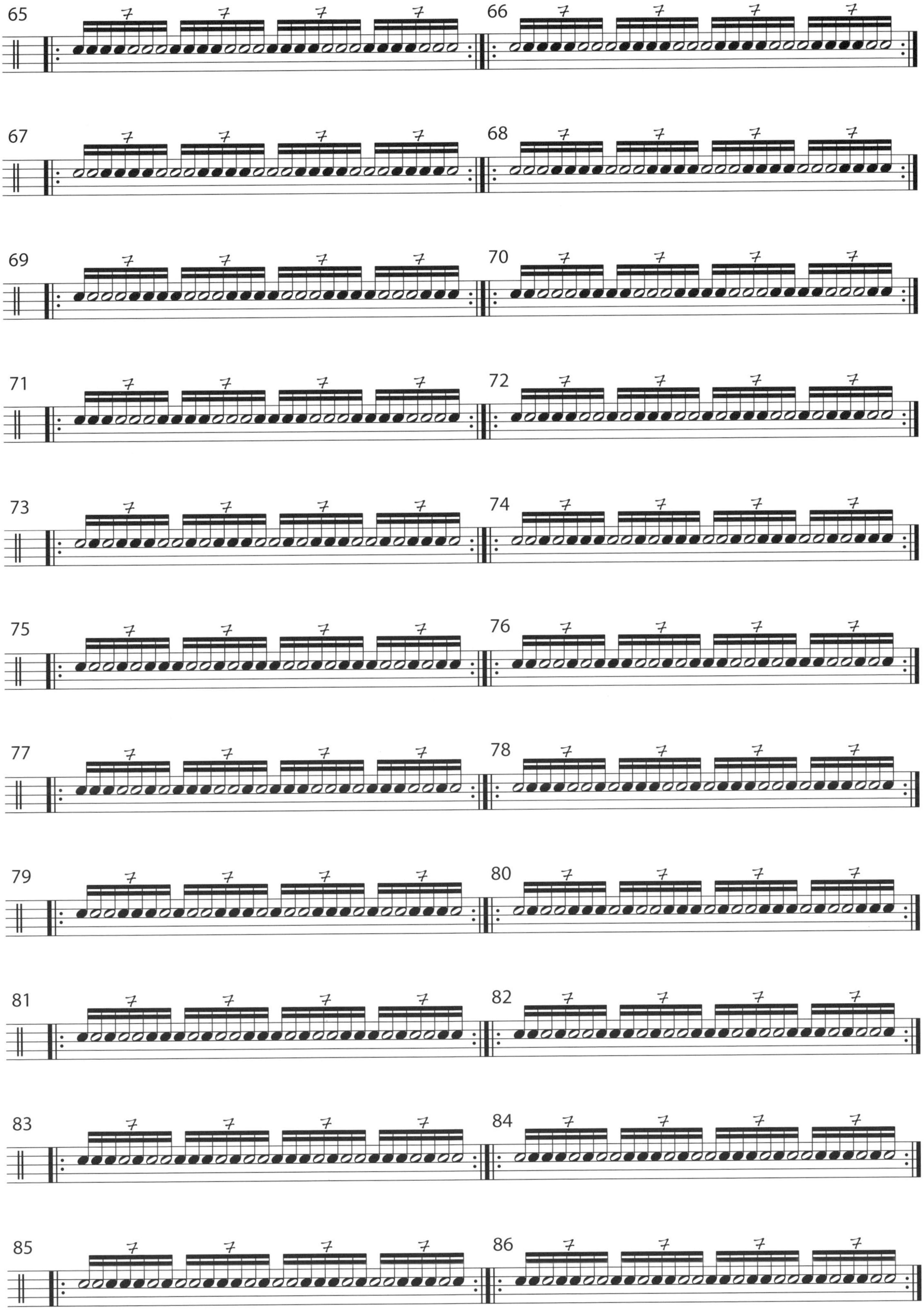
65
66
67
68
69
70
71
72
73
74
75
76
77
78
79
80
81
82
83
84
85
86

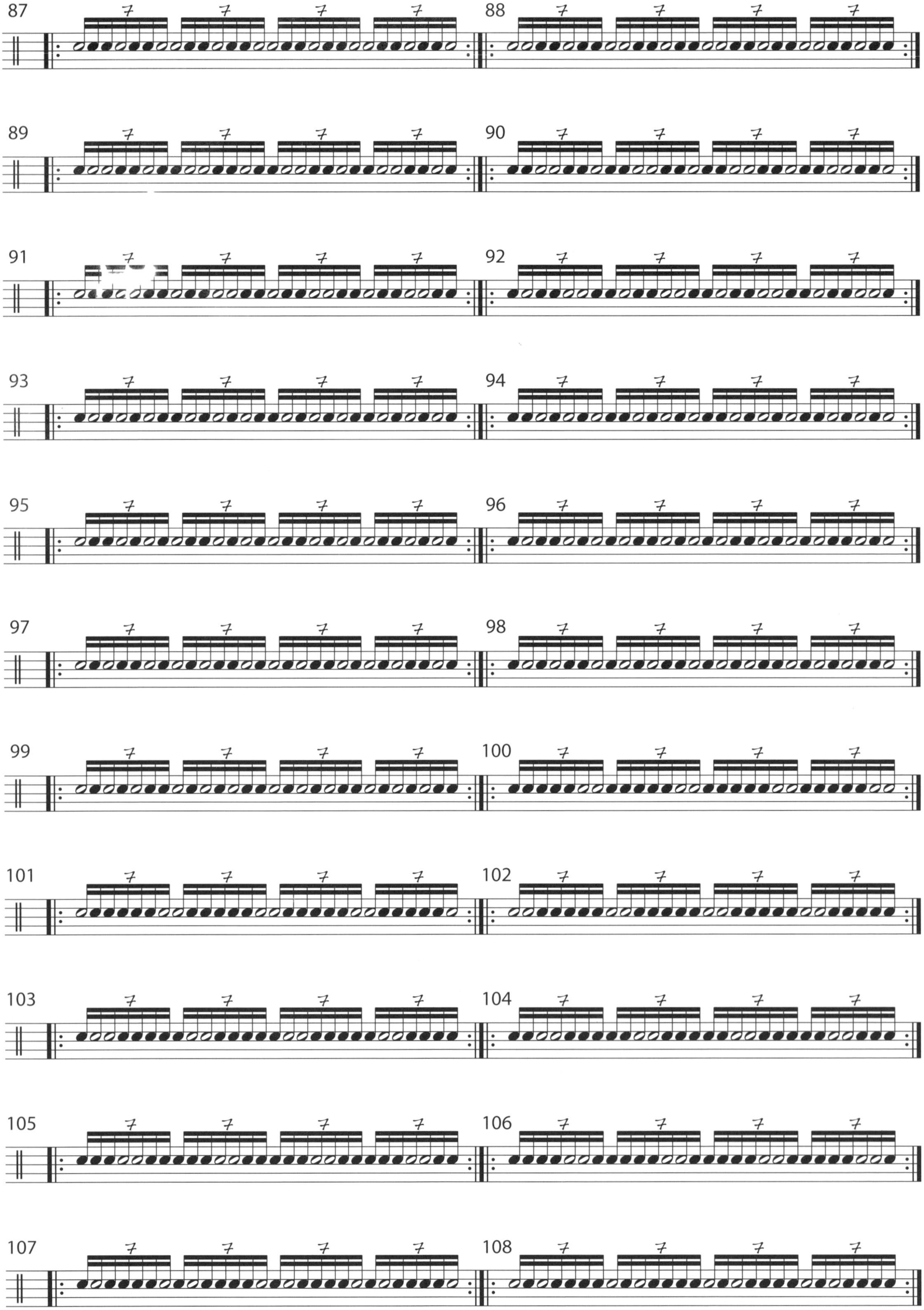
87
88
89
90
91
92
93
94
95
96
97
98
99
100
101
102
103
104
105
106
107
108

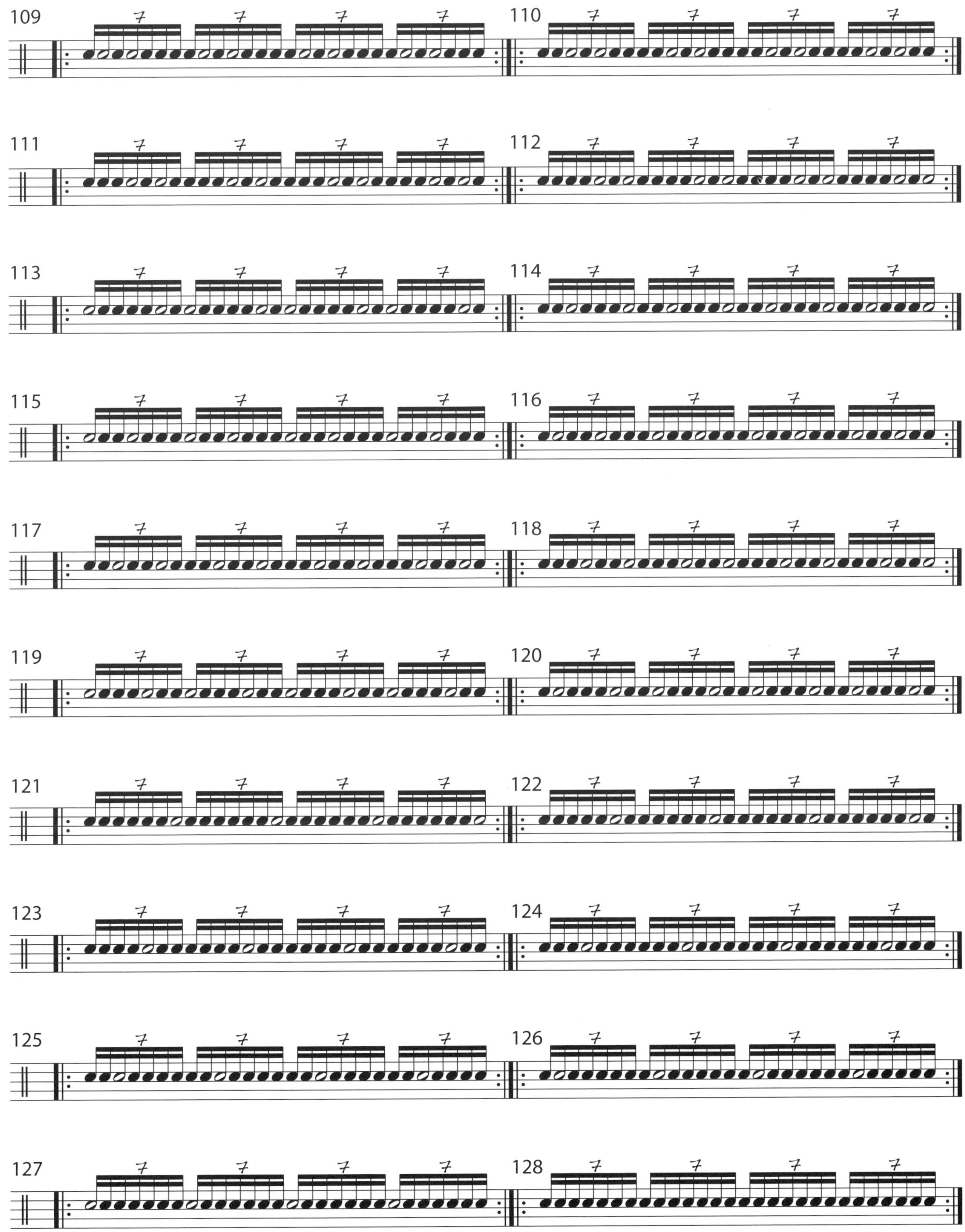
109
110
111
112
113
114
115
116
117
118
119
120
121
122
123
124
125
126
127
128

The Key to Displacements / Polymetric

Accent displacements and **polyrhythms / polymeters** are two thematic areas that have now become almost commonplace in modern percussion playing.

This chapter will reveal the close connection between these two areas and how to progress from **polyrhythms / polymeters** to **accent displacements** and vice versa.

Displacements

The first set of exercises concentrates on the execution of accent displacements in groups of 3, 5, and 7 ranging from eighth notes to thirty-second-notes.

The note value associated with the relevant numerical value or note values that can be divided by this numerical value will not be played. This means that in the accent displacements in groupings of three, both triplets and sixteenth-note triplets will be omitted. In the accent displacements in groupings of five, quintuplets will be omitted, and in the groupings of seven, the septuplets.

Rule

Each accent displacement requires the same number of bars to return to the first bar in the beat as expressed by its number—this is generally valid for all note values.

Accent displacements in groupings of three therefore require three bars in a 4/4 time signature to end on the first beat, irrespective of whether these displacements are played in eighths or quintuplets. Displacements in groupings of five require five bars, and for groupings of seven, seven bars.

I suggest that the exercises be played with the following stickings:

RLRL, LRLR, RRLL, LLRR, RLLR, and LRRL.

The accents can in turn also be interpreted. I recommend that the **unaccented** beats be played as **ghost notes**.

Ex.:

Displacements in 3

Displacements in 3: Eighth Notes

Displacements in 3: Sixteenth Notes

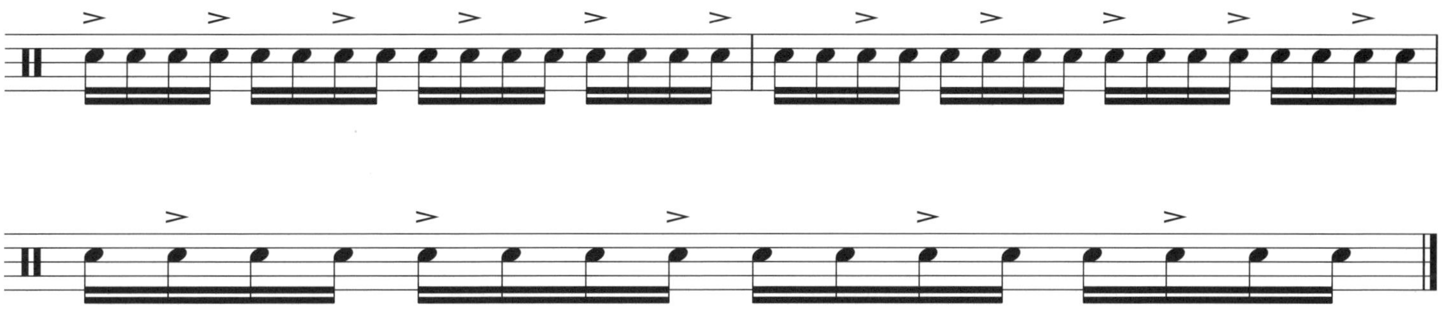

Displacements in 3: Quintuplets

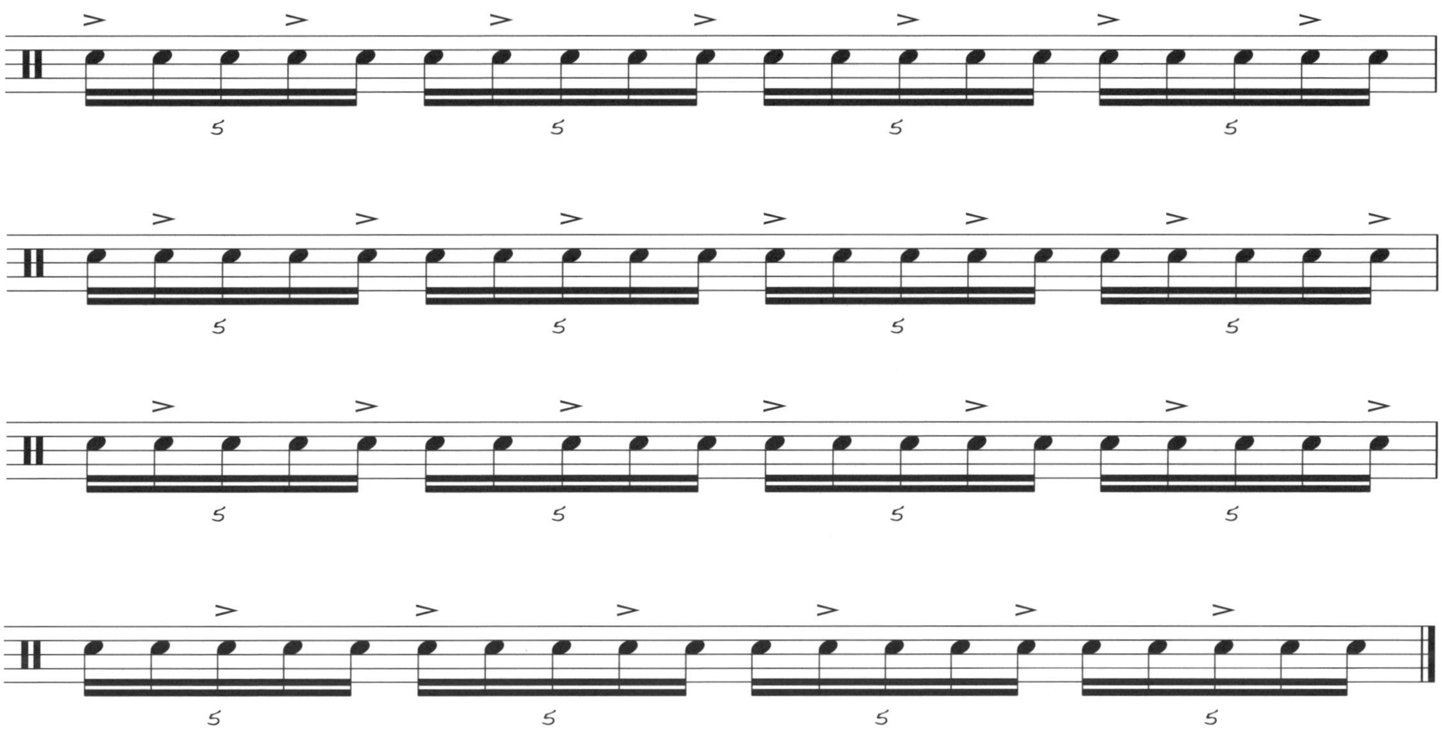

Displacements in 3: Septuplets

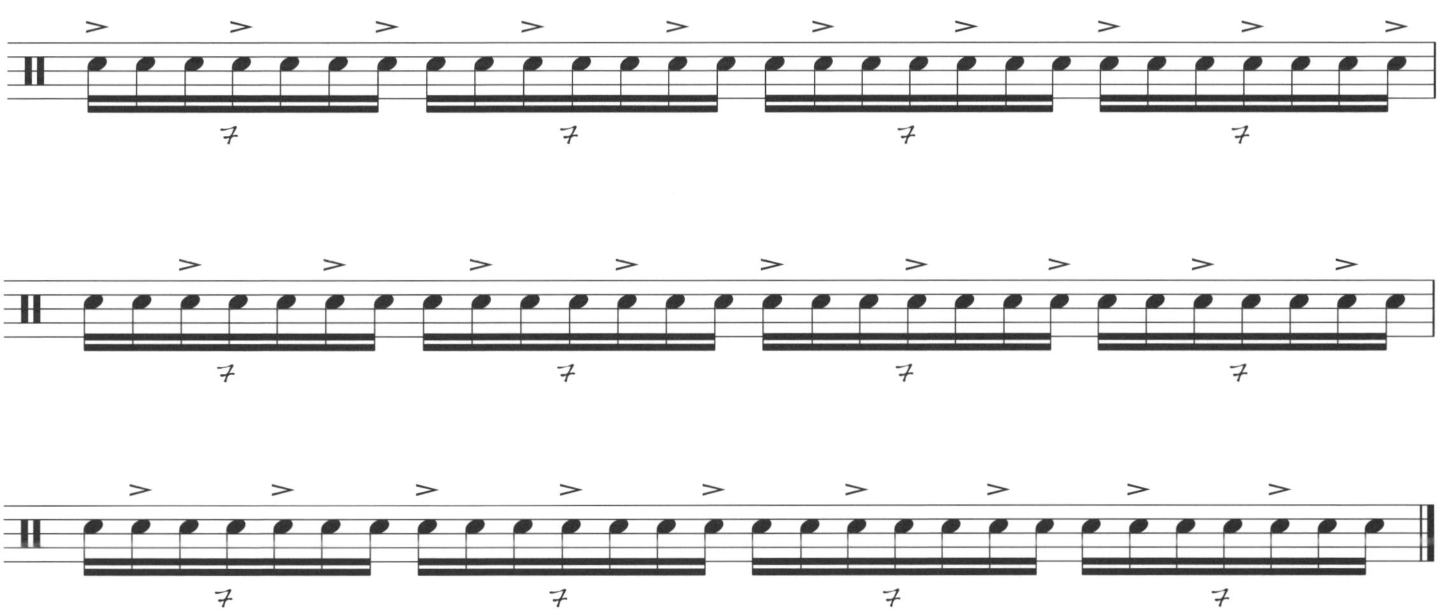

Displacements in 5

Displacements in 5: Eighth Notes

Displacements in 5: Eighth-Note Triplets

Displacements in 5: Sixteenth Notes

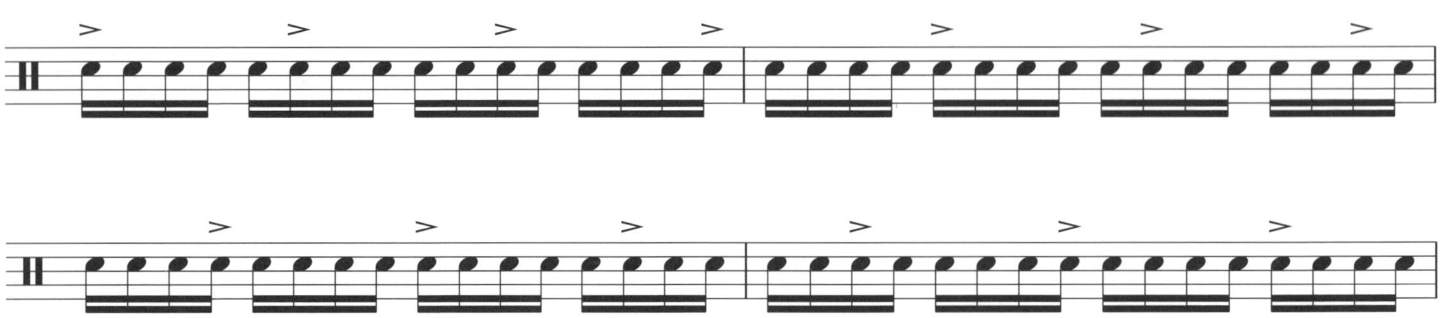

Displacements in 5: Sextuplets

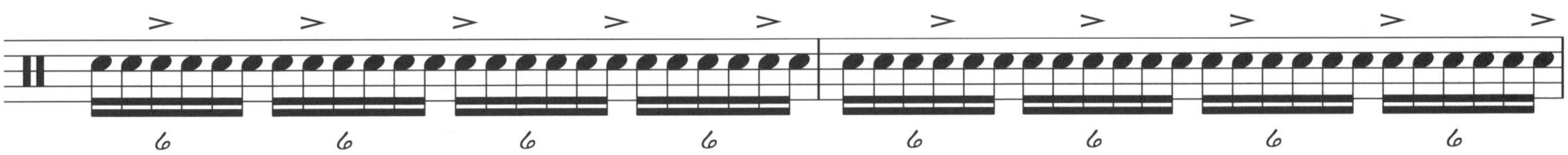

Displacements in 5: Septuplets

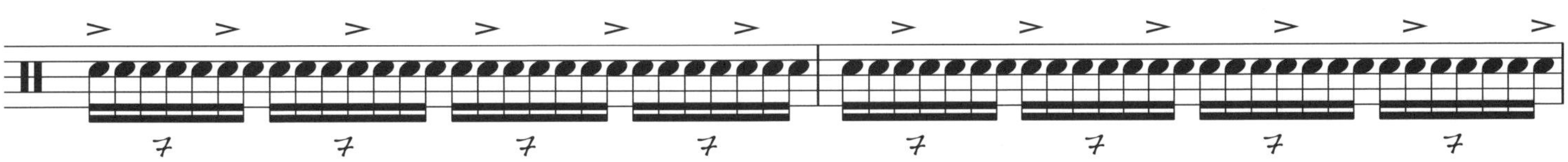

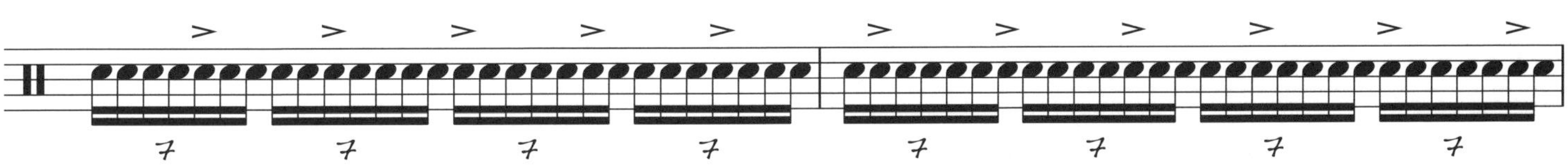

Displacements in 7

Displacements in 7: Eighth Notes

Displacements in 7: Eighth-Note Triplets

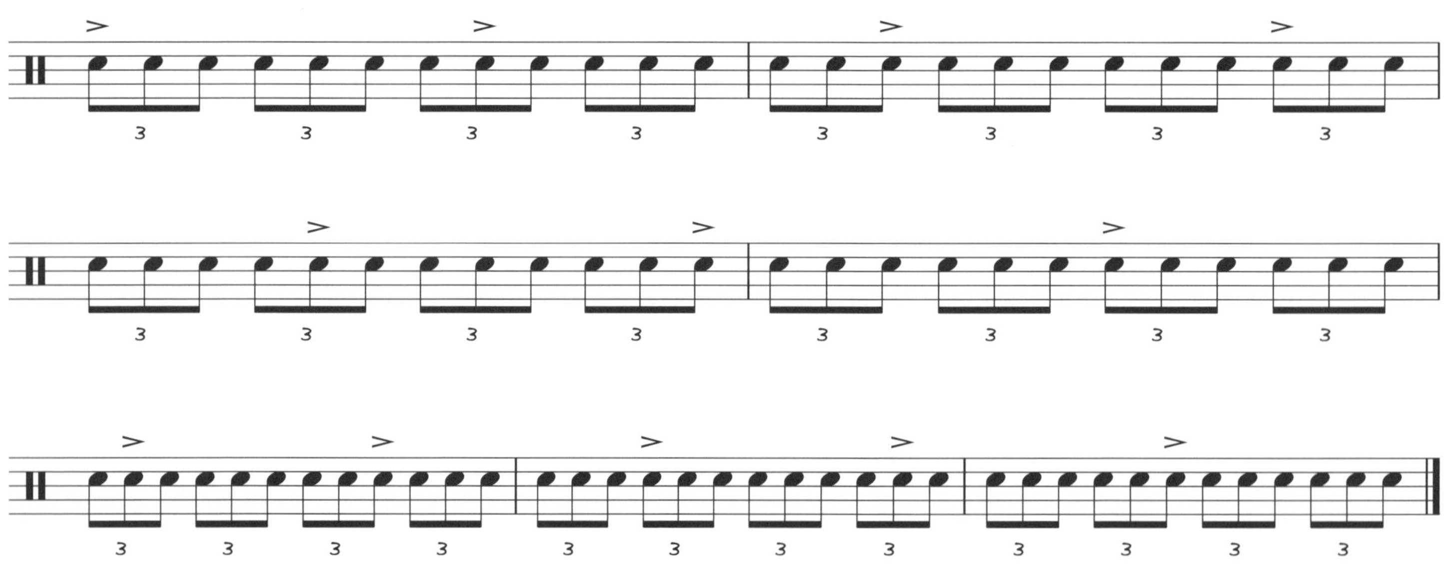

Displacements in 7: Sixteenth Notes

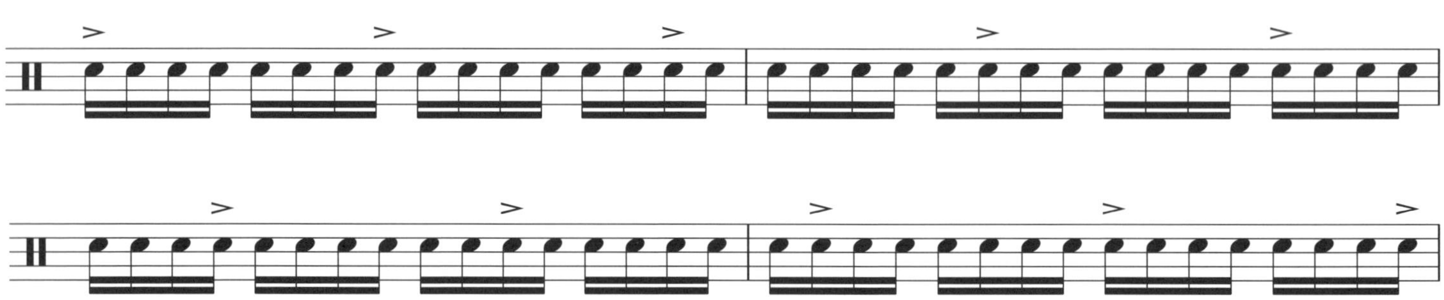

Displacements in 7: Quintuplets

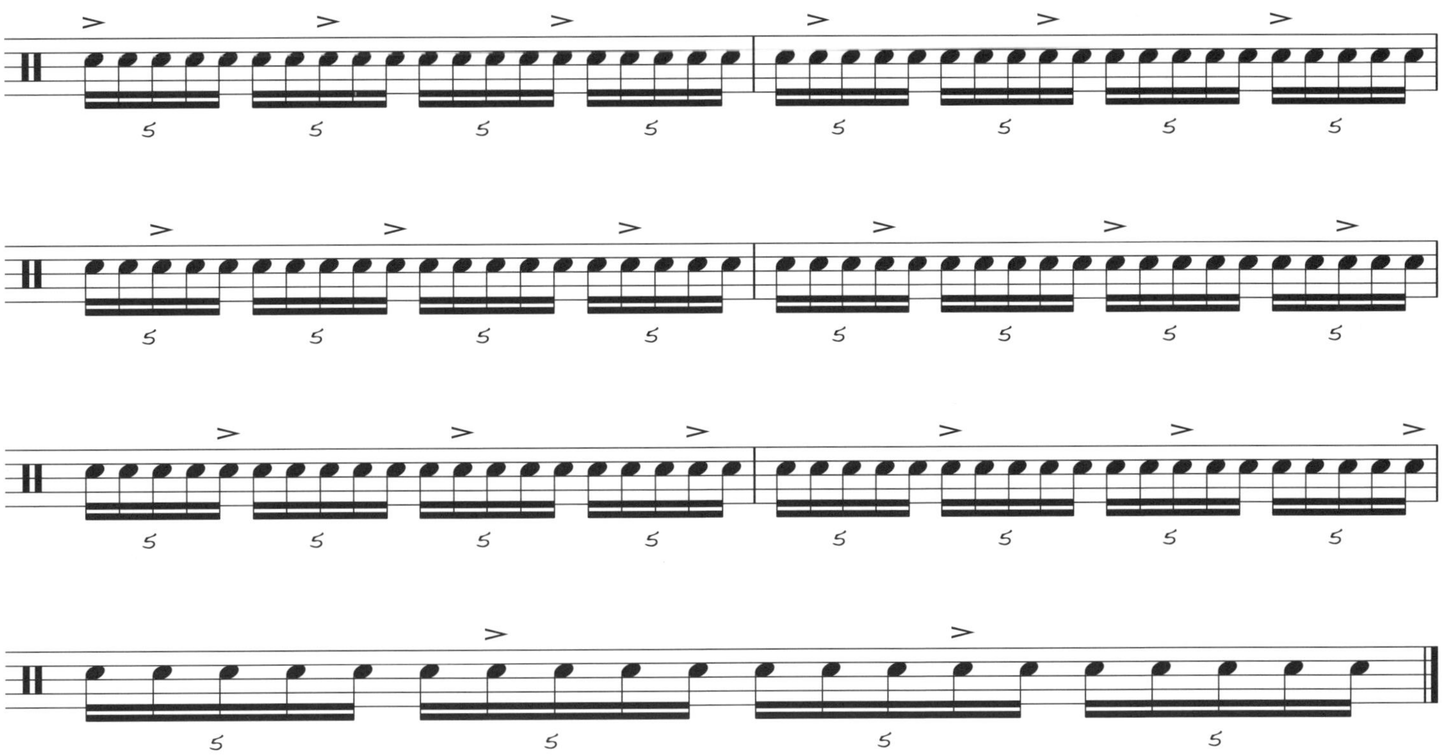

Displacements in 7: Sextuplets

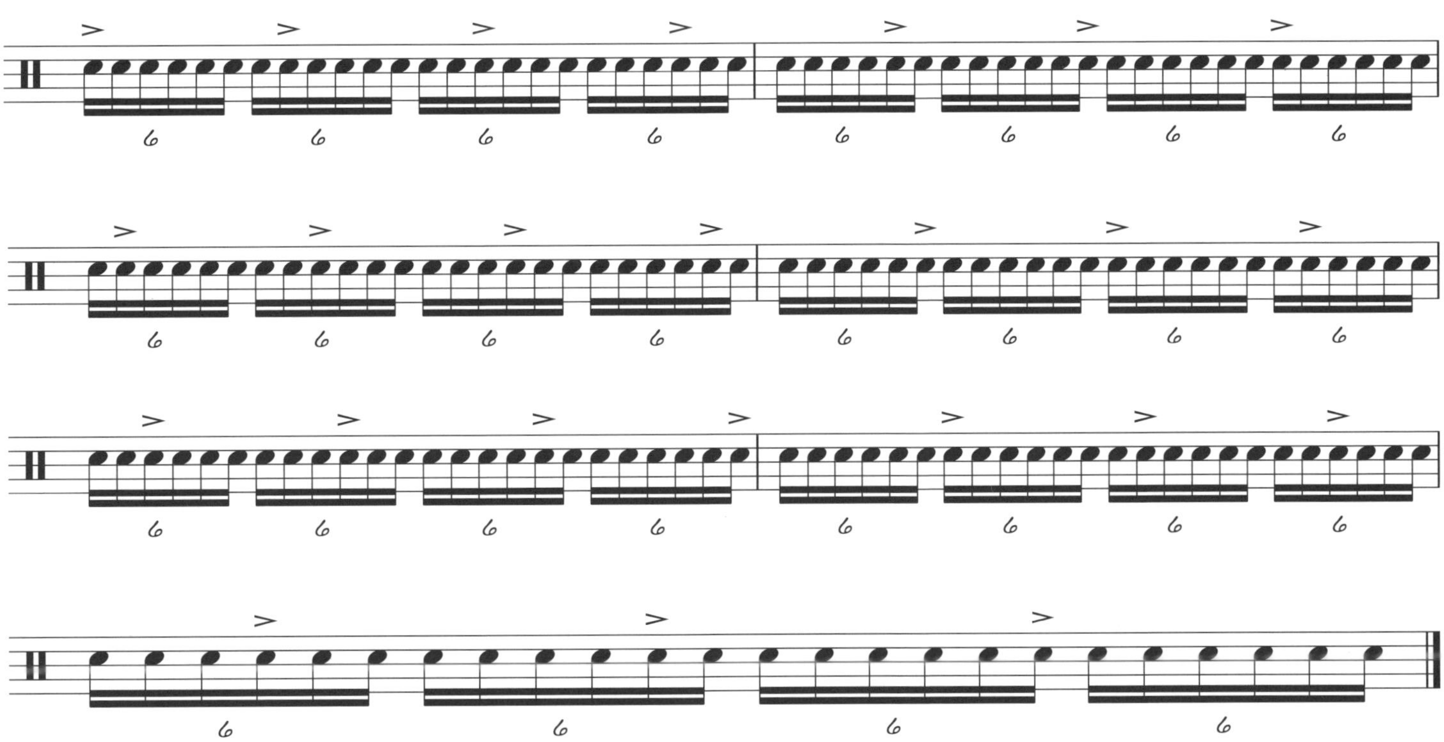

Polyrhythms / Polymetric

In order to understand the concept of **polyrhythms / polymetrics** and subsequently employ this feature when playing music, it is important to utilize the principle of accent displacement. Here it is important to adhere to the following rule:

Rule

To achieve the retention of two different superimposed meters in a single bar, it is first necessary to determine the appropriate time signature. This is dictated by the first meter—the second meter is achieved through an accompanying accent displacement.

If, for example, you want to play three against two, you must first choose a time signature. In this case it would be 2/4. The accent displacement leading to the triple meter is produced by playing the eighth-note triplets with a displacement in groupings of two.

Below you will find the application possibilities for polymeters over groupings of **two, three,** and **four**.

Polyrhythms / Polymetric Over 2

3 Over 2:

5 Over 2:

7 Over 2:

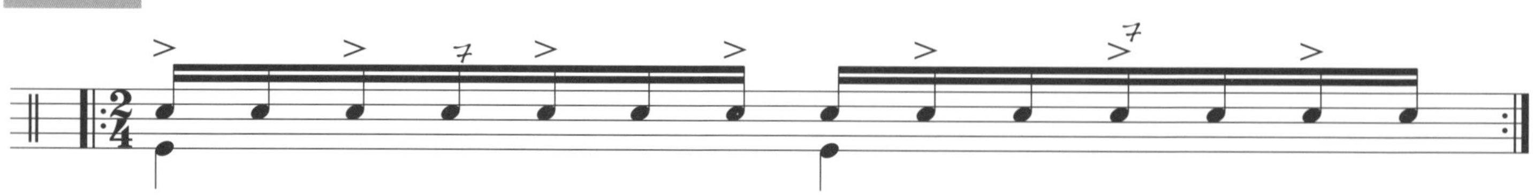

Polyrhythms / Polymetric Over 3

2 Over 3:

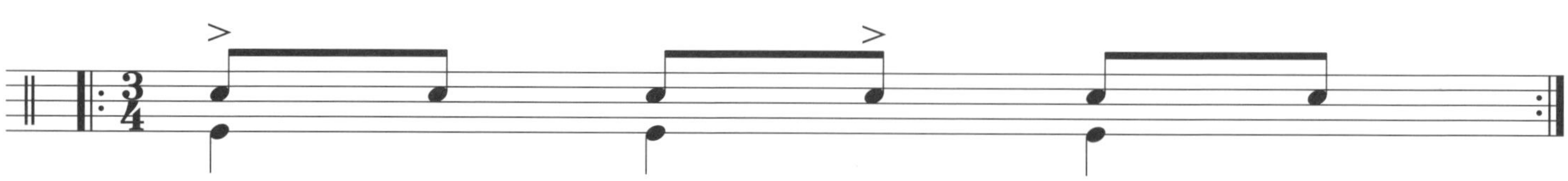

4 Over 3:

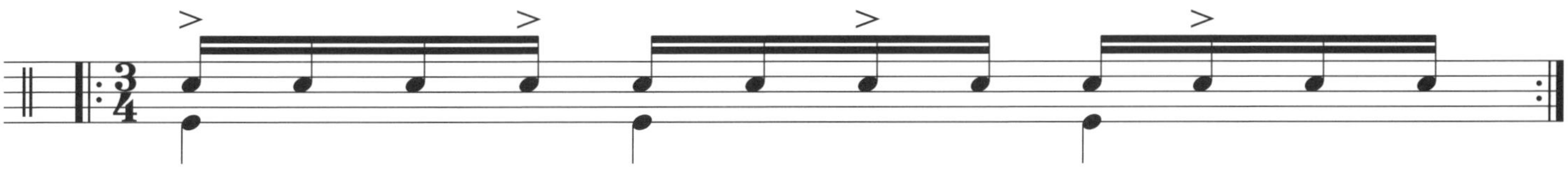

5 Over 3:

7 Over 3:

Polyrhythms / Polymetric Over 4

3 Over 4:

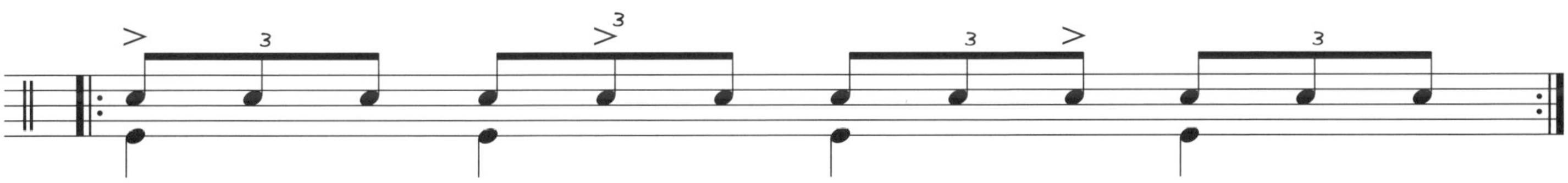

5 Over 4:

7 Over 4:

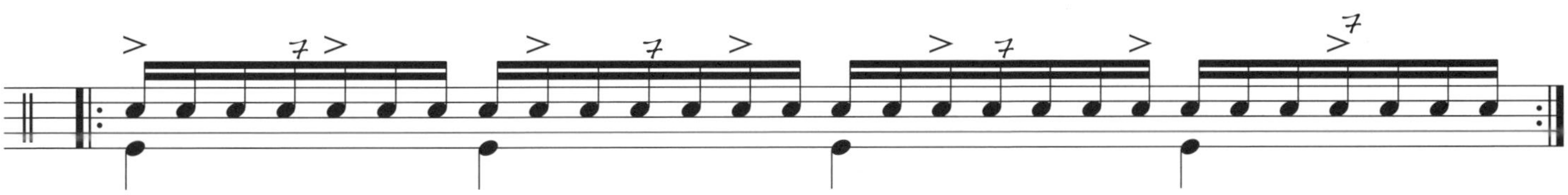

Your Own Key

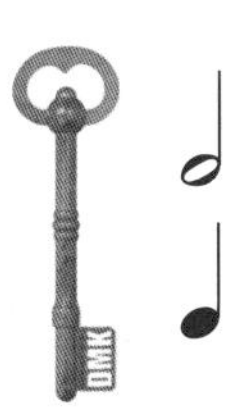

More Products by F.A.Z.!

Daily Drumset Workout

Original Classics of Drum Literature